Teach English

A training course for teachers

Teacher's Workbook

Adrian Doff

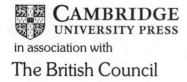

CAMBRIDGE
UNIVERSITY PRESS
in association with
The British Council

Published by the Press Syndicate of the University of Cambridge
The Pitt Building, Trumpington Street, Cambridge CB2 1RP
40 West 20th Street, New York, NY 10011–4211, USA
10 Stamford Road, Oakleigh, Victoria 3166, Australia

Text © The British Council 1988
Illustrations © Cambridge University Press 1988

First published 1988
Eight printing 1994

Printed in Great Britain
by Scotprint Ltd, Musselburgh, Scotland

Library of Congress catalog card number: 87–25583

British Library cataloguing in publication data

Doff, Adrian

Teach English: a training course for
teachers.
1. English language – Study and teaching
– Foreign speakers
I. Title
428.2′4′07   PE1128.A2

ISBN 0 521 34863 3 Teacher's Workbook
ISBN 0 521 34864 1 Trainer's Handbook

Contents

Introduction

To the teacher

Teach English is a teacher training course which develops practical skills in teaching English as a foreign language. The course contains 24 units. Each unit focusses on a different area of methodology, and provides about four hours of training material. The units cover a wide range of teaching skills and techniques: basic classroom skills (presenting, eliciting, organising practice, correcting errors); practical techniques for developing listening, speaking, reading and writing; use of aids and materials (the blackboard, other visual aids, workcards); and skills of preparation and evaluation.

This is the *Teacher's Workbook* accompanying the course. Each unit in the Workbook contains five or six activities, which you will follow in the training session under the trainer's guidance. These activities take the form of discussion, practice and simple workshop tasks, and are designed to help you develop insights into teaching methods as well as to give you practice in teaching techniques. The final activity in each unit is 'Lesson preparation', which will give you an opportunity to apply techniques from the training course to one of your own lessons. This is followed by a 'Self-evaluation sheet', which you can use to help you reflect on your own teaching after the training session.

This Workbook also contains four 'Background texts', which deal with more theoretical aspects of language teaching. These appear after every fifth unit, but can be read at any point in the course.

At the end of the Workbook, there are brief summaries of each unit for reference.

1 Presenting vocabulary

1 Introduction

Here are some techniques for teaching new words.

Say the word clearly and write it on the board.
Get the class to repeat the word in chorus.
Translate the word into the students' own language.
Ask students to translate the word.
Draw a picture to show what the word means.
Give an English example to show how the word is used.
Ask questions using the new word.

Which are the most useful techniques?
Can you think of any other techniques you could use?

2 Giving examples

1. The examples beside the six words below are not enough to make the
   meaning of the words clear. *Add* one or two sentences to each one, so that
   the meaning of the word is shown clearly.
   a) *market*   You can buy food at the market.
   b) *clothes*   In the morning we put on our clothes.
   c) *noisy*   Students are often very noisy.
   d) *look for*   I'm looking for my pen.
   e) *visit*   Last weekend I visited my uncle.
   f) *happiness* He was full of happiness.
   g) *impossible* Your plan is quite impossible.

2. What *other* techniques could you use (pictures, mime, etc.) to make the
   meaning of each word clearer?

3 Combining different techniques

Look at these words. Decide exactly how you would present each one. If possible,
think of a *variety* of techniques.

laugh   absent   cheese   cold   apron   wall

4   Using a new word

A. The teacher has just presented the word 'market'. Now she is asking
    questions using the new word. What is the purpose of this?

B. Think of two or three questions you could ask the class, using these words.

to cook   lion   holiday   magazine   windy

5   Vocabulary expansion

1. Look at these sets of words. How are the words in each box related to 'cook'?

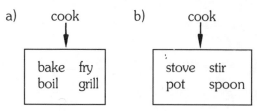

2. Imagine you are teaching the words below.
    Think of four or five other related words that you could teach at the same
    time.
    a) thief
    b) carpet
    c) customs officer
    d) marry

6   Active and passive vocabulary

In Britain, the weather is very varied; people never know what it will be like the next day.

The summer is warmer than the winter, but even in summer the average temperature is only 16°. Sometimes the sun shines, but at other times the sky is covered in cloud, and it often rains.

In winter it is sometimes very cold, especially in the north of the country. The temperature may fall below 0°, and then there is often snow and ice.

The best season of the year is probably late spring. At this time of year the weather is often sunny and quite warm; the countryside looks very green, and there are wild flowers everywhere.

(adapted from a text from *The Cambridge English Course* Book 1: M. Swan and C. Walter)

1. Imagine you want to present these new words from the text.
   weather   varied   average   temperature   cloud   snow
   ice   season   spring   sunny   countryside
   Which words would you present as *active* vocabulary, and which would you present as *passive* vocabulary? Write the words in *two lists*.
2. How would you *present* the words?

---

7   Lesson preparation

---

1. Choose a lesson which you will teach soon, or find a lesson in a suitable textbook. Identify the new vocabulary. Choose the most important words which you would focus on as active vocabulary.
2. Prepare:
   – a presentation of each word, to show its meaning;
   – a few questions to ask, using each word.
3. Look at the other new vocabulary in the lesson. Decide how you would teach it.

Self-evaluation sheet

Complete this after you have taught the lesson.

Write down the main new words you taught in the lesson.

What techniques did you use to present them?

a)

b)

c)

d)

e)

f)

Think about these questions.

Which techniques were the most successful? Why?
Which were the least successful? Why?

Did you use any new techniques for the first time?

If so, did they make the lesson better or worse? In what way?

Did you ask any questions during your presentation?
What replies did students give?

How much time did you spend in the lesson on presenting vocabulary?
Do you think this was: too much? too little? the right amount?

What might you do differently next time you present vocabulary?

2 Asking questions

1 Question types

What is the difference between these three types of question?
How might you reply to each question?

a) Do you drink tea?
   Can you swim?
   Did he go to university?
   Are they coming to the party?

b) Do you prefer tea or coffee?
   Are they brothers or just friends?
   Will you walk or go by bus?
   Did she study in Britain or in the United States?

c) What do you usually drink?
   Where did she study?
   How long have they known each other?
   When are you leaving?

2 Checking questions

Imagine that you have just presented each of these words or phrases.
   wide/narrow   belong to   inside/outside   far from   depend on
Write down one or two questions you could ask in class, to check that students
understand each item.

3 Real classroom questions

What questions could you ask in these situations?
a) It's a hot day, and all the windows are closed.
b) One of your students looks pale and tired.
c) You set homework last lesson. Today you are going to check the answers with
   the class.
d) Several students are absent today.
e) When you come into class, you find a bag on your desk.
f) When you come into class, you find a face drawn on the blackboard.

4   Eliciting long answers

A teacher is reviewing a text from an earlier lesson. Now he wants the students to reproduce it in their own words. What prompts or questions could he ask which would naturally lead students to answer with complete sentences from the text?

What did Diana and Peter do?

What about the stairs?

Tell me about the tower.

And at the top?

On their first day in the capital, Diana and Peter visited the Old Tower which stood on a hill near the city centre. There were stairs leading to the top, but Diana and Peter decided to take the lift. At the top there was a café and a balcony where visitors could stand and admire the view. It was magnificent – you could see the whole city, the river and the hills beyond. On their way back from the Tower, Diana and Peter went past the main square in the city centre. They stopped at a stall to have some orange juice, and sat and watched the traffic for a while. The square was very busy, with cars, buses, bicycles and pedestrians going in all directions. In the centre of the square there was a policeman controlling the traffic.

5   Questioning strategies

Here are four different strategies for asking questions in class.

A.

> What's this made of?
> Anyone?

> Wood!

B.

> What's this made of?
> .... Fatma?

> It's made of wood

C.

> Hamdia ... What's this made of?

> It's made of wood

D.

> What's this made of?
> .... Yes. Samia?

> It's made of wood

1. Which of these strategies do you use in your own class? Which do you use most often?
2. What are the advantages and disadvantages of each strategy?
   Consider which strategies:
   - help the teacher to control the class;
   - help to keep the attention of the whole class;
   - give good students a chance to show their knowledge;
   - give weak or shy students a chance to answer;
   - give lazy students a chance *not* to answer.

6   Lesson preparation

1. Choose a lesson which you will teach soon, or find a lesson in a suitable textbook. Focus on one part of the lesson, in which you would want the class to answer questions.
2. Write down all the questions which you plan to ask. Beside each question, write the answer which you hope the students would give.
3. Decide what questioning strategies you would use.

Self-evaluation sheet
Complete this after you have taught the lesson.

Write down questions you asked in the lesson.	What answers did students give?
a)	
b)	
c)	
d)	
e)	
f)	
g)	
h)	

Think about these questions.

Did students give the answers which you expected?
Did they give natural answers?
How many students answered each question?
Were the questions: too easy? too difficult? the right level?

What strategy did you use for asking your questions?
Was the strategy successful, or would a different strategy have been better?

Think of two good students, two average students, and two weak students in your class.
What did each of them *do* during this part of the lesson?

3 Presenting structures

1 Structures and examples

Look at each sentence in turn. Think of two or three more examples of the
structure in italics. Write the examples together in a table.
a) *Shall I* open the window?
b) He *seems to* be rich.
c) *Is there any* tea?
d) I *used to* live in the country.
e) *She's writing* a letter.
f) The room was *so* dark *that* I couldn't see anything.

2 Ways of showing meaning

This is how different teachers presented *comparison of adjectives* to their
students. Which presentation do you think is:
– the most interesting?
– the easiest?
– the most useful?

Teacher A:

I talked about two buildings
in the town. ('The post office
is bigger than the bank.')

Teacher B:

I drew lines on
the board. ('Line A
is longer than Line B.')

-ER THAN
NOT AS . . . AS . . .

Teacher C:

I called a tall and a short
student to the front and
compared them. ('Anna is
taller than Maria.')

Teacher D:

I drew pictures of two men
on the board and
compared them. ('Hani is
taller than Abdou.')

3   Presenting a structure

A teacher presented the structure 'has been . . . -ing . . . for . . .' to her class. To make the meaning clear, she drew pictures on the board and gave this imaginary situation: 'A woman starts waiting for a bus at four o'clock. At five o'clock the bus comes. She's been waiting for an hour.'

Here are the teacher's notes for the lesson, but they are not in their correct order. What order should they be in? Are all the stages necessary?

Say 'She's been waiting for an hour' and ask the class to repeat it phrase by phrase.

Explain how the structure is formed.

Write the sentence on the board:
She's been waiting for an hour.

Give other situations and examples:
Another person arrived at 4.30.
He's been waiting for half an hour.
etc.

Ask the class to copy the sentence.

Ask individual students to repeat the sentence.

Draw pictures to show the situation, and give the example 'She's been waiting for an hour'.

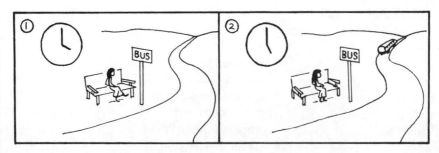

4   Contrasting structures

a) I've got **some** bread. I haven't got **any** bread.
b) I'**ve seen** that film. I **saw** that film last week.
c) If they **build** a reservoir, there **will** be plenty of water.
   If they **built** a reservoir, there **would** be plenty of water.

Discuss each pair of sentences in turn.
– What is the difference between the sentences?
– Can you think of other *examples* which would show the difference?
– How could you *explain* the difference simply to your students, using their own
  language?

5   Lesson preparation

1. Choose a lesson which you will teach soon, or find a lesson in a suitable
   textbook, which introduces a major new structure.
2. How is the structure introduced? Are there enough examples? Would the
   examples be suitable for your class? Can you think of other situations or
   examples to show how the structure is used?
3. Plan a presentation of the structure. Use the notes in Activity 3 to help you
   decide what steps you would include.

Self-evaluation sheet

Complete this after you have taught the lesson.

1. What structure did you present?

2. What examples did you give?

3. Write down the main steps you followed in your presentation.

   a)

   b)

   c)

   d)

   e)

Think about these questions.

How did you add to the presentation in the textbook?
How did the parts that you added improve the presentation?

How much did you involve the class in your presentation?
How many students spoke? What did they say?

By the end of the lesson, could most students:
− understand sentences containing the structure?
− say the structure correctly?
− write the structure correctly?
− use the structure in new contexts?

How did you check that they understood?
Were there any students who didn't understand?
What did you do to help them?

4 Using the blackboard

1 Writing on the blackboard

Both these teachers are presenting language on the blackboard. Which teacher's technique is more effective? Why?

A.

B.

2 Organising the blackboard

Here is a teacher's blackboard at the end of a lesson. How could the layout have been organised more clearly?

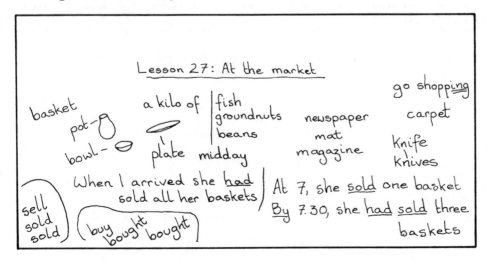

3   Blackboard examples

Look at the examples below.
- What grammar points do they show?
- How would you present them on the blackboard?

a) a book, a table, an egg, an orange.
b) He plays football. Does he play football?
c) shelf, shelves; wife, wives.
d) I haven't seen her for a week. I haven't seen her since Saturday.
e) She is reading. She's reading. He has arrived. He's arrived.
f) He worked so hard that he became ill.

4   Structure tables

I'm You've He's She's We're They've	eating preparing	breakfast lunch dinner

Look at this structure table, which shows forms of the present continuous tense.
1. How could you write the table on the blackboard but still keep the attention of the class?
2. How could you use the table for practice?
3. Design two more structure tables:
    - showing examples with 'How much?' and 'How many?';
    - showing examples of the present perfect tense with 'for' and 'since'.

5   Prompts for practice

Here are three examples of prompts written on the blackboard. What language could each of them be used to practise?

A.

	swim	speak French	dance
Karl	✓	✓	✓
Magda	✗	✓	✗
Anna	✓	✗	✓
You	?	?	?

B.

How many?
doctors   rooms
nurses   blankets
patients   beds

C.

8 o'clock – got up – breakfast –
bus stop – bus – empty – surprised –
school – closed – remembered – holiday

6   Using blackboard drawings

Work in groups. What do these drawings show?

1. Choose *one* of the drawings. Think of a simple story based on it. Think of a series of blackboard drawings which you can use to tell the story (the picture you have chosen will be one of them).
2. Practise drawing the pictures and telling the story.

7   Lesson preparation

1. Choose a lesson which you will teach soon, or find a lesson in a suitable textbook.
2. On a piece of paper, plan exactly what you would write or draw on the blackboard.
   Consider these possibilities:

new words	prompts for practice (words or pictures)
examples of structures	pictures to show the meaning of words
structure tables	pictures to show complete situations

3. Decide what you would say and what the class would do while you were writing on the board.

Self-evaluation sheet

Complete this after you have taught the lesson.

Think about these questions.

1. Look at the list in 'Lesson preparation'. Which of these did you use the blackboard for? Did you use it for any other purpose?
   Did your blackboard look different from the one in your plan? If so, in what ways?
   Think of each student in your class in turn. Could they all read what you wrote on the board? How do you know?

2. If you wrote *vocabulary* on the board:
   – Were the words new to the whole class or only some students?
   – Were all the words you wrote necessary? How did they help the lesson?
   – What did the students do? (read the words? write them down? repeat them?)

3. If you wrote *examples* or *tables* on the board:
   – Think of one good student and one weaker student in your class. What were they doing while you wrote on the board?
   – How did you use the examples (e.g. for practice)?
   – Was it necessary to write the examples on the board? How did it help the lesson?

4. If you drew *pictures* on the board:
   – How much time did you take to draw them?
   – What did the students do while you drew the pictures?
   – Could all the students recognise what the pictures meant?
   – How did you use the pictures?
   – Do you think the pictures helped your lesson? If so, in what way?

Reference sheet: Blackboard drawings

A. *Faces*
   Heads should be large enough to be seen from the back of the class.
   Expression can be indicated by changing the shape of the mouth:

happy   sad   laughing   crying

The direction the speaker is facing can be indicated by changing the nose (this is useful if you want to show two people having a conversation):

Sex or age can be indicated by drawing hair:

B. *Stick figures*
For basic male and female stick figures the body should be about twice as long as the head; the arms are the same length as the body; the legs are slightly longer:

Actions can be indicated by bending the legs and arms:

C. *Places*
Buildings, towns, and directions can be indicated by a combination of pictures and words:

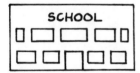  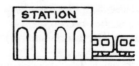 

D. *Vehicles*
Vehicles and movement can be indicated as follows:

5 Using a reading text

1 Reading a text

1. Read the first part of the text silently.

How to get preserved as a fossil

Unfortunately the chances of any animal becoming a fossil are not very great, and the chances of a fossil then being discovered many thousands of years later are even less. It is not surprising that of all the millions of animals that have lived in the past, we actually have fossils of only a very few.

There are several ways in which animals and plants may become fossilised. First, it is essential that the remains are buried, as dead animals and plants are quickly destroyed if they remain exposed to the air. Plants rot, while scavengers, such as insects and hyenas, eat the flesh and bones of animals. Finally, the few remaining bones soon disintegrate in the hot sun and pouring rain. If buried in suitable conditions, however, animal and plant remains will be preserved. The same chemicals which change sand and silt into hard rock will also enter the animal and plant remains and make them hard too. When this happens we say that they have become fossilised. Usually only the bones of an animal and the toughest part of a plant are preserved.

2. Now follow while the trainer reads.

The soft body parts of an animal or the fine fibres of a leaf may occasionally become fossilised, but they must be buried quickly for this to happen. This may sometimes occur with river and lake sediments but is much more likely to happen with volcanic ash. One site near Lake Victoria, where my parents worked, contained many thousands of beautifully preserved insects, spiders, seeds, twigs, roots and leaves. A nearby volcano must have erupted very suddenly, burying everything in a layer of ash. The insects had no time to escape before they were smothered.

Caves are another site where fossils are easily formed, and luckily our ancestors left many clues in caves which made convenient shelters and homes. Things that people brought in as food or tools were left on the cave floor, and they were buried by mud, sand and other debris washed in by rivers and rain.

(from *Human Origins*: R. Leakey)

3. Which technique:
   – makes it easier to understand the text?
   – is more helpful in developing reading ability?

2 New vocabulary

1. Read the text and try to understand the *general meaning* of the story. (All the words in italics are nonsense words.)

> A country girl was walking along the *snerd* with a *roggle* of milk on her head. She began saying to herself, 'The money for which I will sell this milk will make me enough money to increase my *trund* of eggs to three hundred. These eggs will produce the same number of chickens, and I will be able to sell the chickens for a large *wunk* of money. Before long, I will have enough money to live a rich and *fallentious* life. All the young men will want to marry me. But I will refuse them all with a *ribble* of the head – like this . . .'
>
> And as she *ribbled* her head, the *roggle* fell to the ground and all the milk ran in a white stream along the *snerd*, carrying her plans with it.

2. Now look at the nonsense words again. Can you guess what they might mean?

3 Preparing for silent reading

1. The new words are in italics in the text. Write them in two lists:
   – words which you would present before reading;
   – words which you could leave for students to guess, and deal with afterwards.

2. How would you introduce the text? Decide exactly what you would say.

3. Look at these possible guiding questions. Choose the *two* which you think would be best.
   a) Was the doctor rich?
   b) Was the doctor unhappy?
   c) What was the young man's problem?
   d) Where was the man's pain?
   e) What did the doctor advise?

> A doctor who worked in a village was very *annoyed* because many people used to stop him in the street and ask his *advice*. In this way, he was never paid for his *services*, and he never *managed* to earn much money. He *made up his mind* to put an end to this. One day, he was stopped by a young man who said to him, 'Oh, doctor, I'm so glad to see you. I've got a *severe pain* in my left side'. The doctor *pretended* to be interested and said, 'Shut your eyes and *stick* your tongue out of your mouth'. Then he went away, leaving the man standing in the street with his tongue hanging out . . . and a large *crowd* of people laughing at him.

4   Checking comprehension

Look at the text in Activity 3.
Think of a series of short simple questions which you could use to check
comprehension and focus on important words and expressions.
Write them down.

5   Follow-up activities

Any of these activities could be done after reading the text in Activity 3.
Which type of activity do you think is most useful?
Which is least useful?

Discussion questions

Do you think he was a good doctor?
How do you think the young man felt?

Reproducing the text

Tell part of the story from these prompts:
Doctor – village – annoyed.
People – stop – street – advice.
Never paid – never – money.

Role play

Act out the conversation between the doctor and the young man.

Gap-filling

Copy and fill the gaps:
One day, the doctor _____ a young man.
The doctor _____ interested.
He left the man _____ in the street with his tongue _____ out.

6 Lesson preparation

1. Choose a text from the textbook you are using, or from another suitable textbook. If the text is long, choose one part of the text only.
2. Plan part of a lesson, using the text.
   - Decide which words you would present before students read the text.
   - Plan an introduction to the text, and one or two guiding questions.
   - Prepare a series of comprehension questions to ask after the reading, and decide how to present other new words in the text.

Self-evaluation sheet

Complete this after you have taught the lesson.

Write down the main steps you followed in using the text.

a)

b)

c)

d)

e)

Think about these questions.

How did you introduce the text?
How interested were the students in the topic?
Is there any way you could have made them more interested?

What words did you present before students read the text?
Do you think this was: too many? not enough? the right amount?
Think of five *other* new words in the text.
Did most students manage to guess their meaning?

Did you give guiding questions orally or write them on the board?
Did you feel the questions were appropriate?
How many students could answer them?

Was this the first time you asked students to read silently?
If so, how successful was it? Would you organise reading in this way again?

Think of one *fast* reader and one *slow* reader in your class.
What did they each do during the reading phase?
How did you keep them both involved?

By the end of the whole activity:
– How many students do you think fully understood the text?
– Were most students still interested in the topic?

Think of two *weak* students and two *good* students.
What did they learn from this lesson?

Background text: Reading

Before you read:

Here are some statements about reading. Do you think they are true or false?

1. Silent reading involves looking at a text and saying the words silently to yourself.
2. There are no major differences between how one reads in one's mother tongue and how one reads in a foreign language.
3. To understand a word, you have to read all the letters in it; to understand a sentence, you have to read all the words in it.
4. The teacher can help students to read a text by reading it aloud while they follow in their books.

Now read the text:

If we are to help students develop reading skills in a foreign language, it is important to understand what is involved in the reading process itself. If we have a clear idea of how 'good readers' read, either in their own or a foreign language, this will enable us to decide whether particular reading techniques are likely to help learners or not.

In considering the reading process, it is important to distinguish between two quite separate activities: *reading for meaning* (or 'silent reading') and *reading aloud*. Reading for meaning is the activity we normally engage in when we read books, newspapers, road signs, etc.; it is what you are doing as you read this text. It involves looking at sentences and understanding the message they convey, in other words 'making sense' of a written text. It does not normally involve saying the words we read, not even silently inside our heads; there are important reasons for this, which are outlined below.

Reading aloud is a completely different activity; its purpose is not just to understand a text but to convey the information to someone else. It is not an activity we engage in very often outside the classroom; common examples are reading out parts of a newspaper article to a friend, or reading a notice to other people who cannot see it. Obviously, reading aloud involves looking at a text, understanding it and also saying it. Because our attention is divided between reading and speaking, it is a much more difficult activity than reading silently; we often stumble and make mistakes when reading aloud in our own language, and reading aloud in a foreign language is even more difficult.

When we read for meaning, we do not need to read every letter of every word, nor even every word in each sentence. This is because, provided the text makes sense, we can guess much of what it says as we read it. To see how this happens at the level of individual words, try reading this sentence:

A m–– was walk––– d––n the s––––t, c–r––ing a gr––n –––––––.

Even though more than half the letters were missing, you could probably read the sentence without difficulty, and even guess the last word without the help of any letters. You may also have noticed that as soon as you guessed the second word, it helped you to guess the whole of the first part of the sentence. This example is an isolated sentence; if you are reading connected sentences in a text, each sentence helps you to guess what the next one will be, and so on through the whole text. Reading is an active process. When we read, we do not merely sit there as passive 'receivers' of the text; we also draw on our own knowledge of the world and of language to help us guess what the text will say next. It is only if we are reading a series of words that makes no sense at all, such as:

Man walking elephant the onto reading to help

that we have to slow down and read every single word, as we can no longer make guesses.

Normally when we read our eyes take in whole phrases at a time; they do not move from word to word in a straight line, but flick backwards and forwards over the text. You can easily test this for yourself. Try covering a text with a piece of paper and reading it literally word by word, moving the paper along from each word to the next. You will probably find that you soon lose track of the meaning, and you need to keep looking back to take in whole sentences. This highlights another important aspect of reading: it is not just that we do not need to read word by word, but rather that it is almost impossible to read and understand a text in this way. Attempting to read one word at a time slows down reading so much that we lose the sense of what we are reading.

There are of course differences between reading in our own language, where comprehension does not usually pose a problem, and reading a foreign language, and the differences are even greater if the foreign language uses a different writing system. But the characteristics of 'good reading' are the same in any language, and in developing reading skills we need to be sure we are not hindering our students but helping them to become good readers, efficient at extracting meaning from written texts.

Discussion

Look again at the statements at the beginning. Are your answers still the same?

6 Practising structures

1 From presentation to practice

Here is part of a teacher's lesson plan.

Aim: To teach Ss to make suggestions using 'Let's . . .'.

Presentation
1. Give a situation and example:
   You're sitting at home with a friend. You can't decide what to do. You suggest different things. For example, you want to watch television – so you say 'Let's watch television'.
2. Chorus repetition:
   Let's watch television.
   Write the sentence on the board.

What should the teacher do next? Consider these possibilities.

Repetition

T: Let's play football.
Ss: Let's play football.
T: Let's go swimming.
Ss: Let's go swimming.
    etc.

Substitution

T: You want to play football.
Ss: Let's play football.
T: You want to go swimming.
Ss: Let's go swimming.

⟫→

Single word prompts

T: cinema
Ss: Let's go to the cinema.
T: football
Ss: Let's play football.

Free substitution

Students make up their own
sentences, e.g.:
Let's go fishing.

Picture prompts

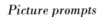

---

2 Meaningful practice

Do each pair of exercises. How are exercise (a) and exercise (b) different?

1a.

> Anne likes *tea* but she doesn't
> like *coffee*.
>
> a) folk music/pop music
> b) walking/swimming
> c) cats/dogs
>   . . .   . . .

1b.

> Say *true* sentences about yourself:
>   I like tea.
> *or* I don't like tea.
>
> What about: a) coffee?
>   b) pop music?
>   c) cats?
>   . . .

2a.

> You are a stranger. Ask about
> places in the town.
>
> a café:
> Is there a café near here?
>
> a) a grocer's shop
> b) a cinema
> c) a fruit stall
>   . . .

2b.

> You are a stranger. Ask about
> places in the town.
>
> You want to see a film:
> Is there a cinema near here?
>
> a) You want to buy some fruit.
> b) You want to post a letter.
> c) You want to spend the night
>   here.
>   . . .

3a.

> 'Where are you going?'
> 'I'm going to the station.'
>
> a) cinema
> b) zoo
> c) river
>   . . .

3b.

> 'Where are you going?'
> 'I'm going to the station.'
> 'Why?'
> 'Because (I want to buy a train ticket).'
>
> a) cinema
> b) zoo
> c) river
>   . . .

3   Organising practice in class

Here is an exercise practising questions and answers with 'can'.

Can you . . .
  swim?
  drive a car?
  ride a horse?
	Yes, I can.

speak English?
  stand on your head?
  sing?
  fly?
	No, I can't

Here is a possible lesson plan:
– Ask the students to close their books. Read out the questions and answers, and ask the students to repeat them.
– Ask the questions, and the students reply 'Yes, I can' or 'No, I can't'.
– Then the students open their books. Students read out questions in turn, and other students answer.

Comment on the lesson plan. What improvements would you suggest?

4   Free oral practice

1. Talk about *one* of these topics.
   - What are you going to do at the weekend? What about your family and friends?
   - Choose one person in the class. Imagine it is his/her birthday soon. Everyone is going to give a present. Say what present you are going to give, and why.
   - Look at the picture of the farmers on page 66. Imagine what they are each going to do when they arrive home.

2. Could you use this activity in your own class? How would you organise it?

5   Lesson preparation

1. Choose a lesson which you will teach soon, or find a lesson in a suitable textbook, which includes structure practice.
2. Look at the exercises in the textbook. Do they give enough practice? Is the practice meaningful? Is it interesting? Do you need to improve it or add to it in any way?
3. Plan part of a lesson, practising the structure.
   Make sure that:
   - some of the practice is meaningful;
   - at the end of the practice, students have a chance to use the structure more freely in sentences of their own.

Self-evaluation sheet
Complete this after you have taught the lesson.

1. What structure did you practise?

2. Write down the main steps you followed.

   a)

   b)

   c)

   d)

   e)

Think about these questions.

Look again at the steps you followed.
How much of the practice was mechanical?
How much was meaningful?

In general, do you think the students found the practice: too easy? about right? too difficult?

Did any students make mistakes?
What were the main ones?
How did you correct them?

Think of one student at the back of the class, one in the middle, and one at the front.
How many times did each student use the structure?

Think of the free practice at the end.
How many students made sentences using the structure?
What was the most interesting sentence?

7   Using visual aids

1   Introduction

1. Which of these visual aids have you used in your own teaching?
2. How exactly have you used them?

a)	Yourself	
b)	The blackboard	
c)	Real objects	
d)	Flashcards	
e)	Pictures and charts	
f)	Others	

2   Using real objects

Prepositions of place: in, on, beside, between, etc.

Present perfect tense (have just . . . -ed)

Is there . . . ?
Are there . . . ?

X is made of . . .

Expressions of colour, shape, size.

Imagine that you have these real objects available in your classroom. Which ones could you use to practise the language in the circles?

3   Using flashcards

A. Here are two sets of flashcards. What language could you practise using each set?

B. Think of four other objects that could replace 'broom' or 'knife' in the dialogues below.

Copy the pictures of the broom and the knife onto flashcards. Then make four more flashcards showing the other objects.

4   Using charts

Can you think of pictures or diagrams which would make these texts clearer and more interesting?
Design a *chart* to accompany each text.

A.

One day, Paula and Richard decided to make a kite. First they went out and found two straight sticks of the same length. They brought them back home and tied them with a piece of string into the shape of a cross. Then they took some more string and used it to tie the four ends of the sticks together. Then, they spread some brightly coloured paper over the frame and glued it around the string. They stuck a tail made of paper to one of the corners, and tied a long string to the centre of the kite. On the next windy day, they took the kite to a hill near their house and flew it.

B.

In order to stay healthy it is important to have a balanced diet – in other words, food that contains something from each of the three main groups of food. These groups are protein, carbohydrate, and fat.

Proteins are very important for building our bodies; they help us to build new cells as old ones die. Meat and dairy products are major sources of protein, but not the only ones – we can also get protein from fish, eggs and beans.

Carbohydrate and fat are important to enable us to store energy – they provide fuel for the body. Carbohydrates are found in sugar, and in cereals such as rice, maize and wheat. Fats are found in vegetable oil, in butter, and in nuts.

Our body also needs minerals, such as iron and calcium, and vitamins. Fish, vegetables and milk contain most of the minerals we need. Vitamins are found in fresh vegetables and fruit.

(based on texts from *Living English* Book 3: H.M. Abdoul-Fetouh et al.)

5   Lesson preparation

1. Look at lessons you will teach soon, or look at a series of lessons in a suitable textbook. Find places where visual aids would be useful (but where there are no visuals in the textbook). Think about visual aids that might help you to:

    present new vocabulary or structures   practise vocabulary or structures
    introduce a new topic   review language from previous
    introduce a text   lessons

2. Plan *two* different uses of visual aids. Use any of the aids introduced in this unit.

Self-evaluation sheet

Complete this after you have taught the lesson.

Which two kinds of visual aids did you use? Describe briefly what they were and what you used them for.

a)

b)

For each of the visual aids you used, think about these questions.

In general, how much better was your lesson because you used visual aids? Much better? a bit better? about the same? worse?
Why?

Did you use a large picture or chart? If so:
– How did you display it?
– Was your method of display successful?

Did you use drawings or pictures? If so:
– Think of one student at the front, one at the side, and one at the back of your class.
– Could they all see?
– Did they all understand?
– What did they each do during this part of the lesson?

How much time did you spend preparing the visual aid?
Do you expect to use it again? What will you use it for?
Is there another teacher in the school who might use it?

8 Planning a lesson

1 Using the teacher's notes

Does your textbook have teacher's notes?
If so, look at the notes for one lesson.

Do the notes clearly tell you:

	Yes	No
a) the aims of the lesson?		
b) what language is taught in the lesson?		
c) the main stages of the lesson?		
d) how to teach the lesson?		

2 Aims of the lesson

A. Here is part of a first year lesson. Students ask and answer questions from the table, then ask other questions.

When do you When does your friend	get up? eat breakfast? wash? go to school? finish school? go to bed? sleep?	In the morning. In the afternoon. In the evening. At night.

When do you clean your teeth?
      meet your friends?
      play games?
      learn English?		

(adapted from *Welcome to English* Book 1: M. Bates and J. Higgens)

What seems to be the *aim* of the lesson?

B. Three different teachers are about to teach the lesson. Compare their comments.

'What are you going to teach today?'

Teacher A:

We're doing Lesson 15.
It's question and answer practice
using a substitution table.

Teacher B:

We're going to practise
present simple questions with
'When . . .', and time expressions.

Teacher C:

We're going to practise asking
and answering questions using the
present simple, so that students learn
to talk about *everyday activities* and
when they do them.

Which teacher has the clearest idea of the *aim* of the lesson?

3   Stages of the lesson

1. Two teachers describe lessons they gave. For the first one, match the description with the lesson stages in the box.

'Well, first we talked a bit about deserts, and what it's like to travel across a desert. Then we read a text about an explorer who's crossed every desert in the world, and the students answered questions on it. In the text, there were several examples of the present perfect tense; I wrote some of these on the board, and I gave a few more examples orally. Then we did a grammar exercise in the textbook. After that, I asked students to make up their own questions using "Have you ever . . .?", to ask each other.'

1. Introduction.

2. Reading.

3. Presentation.

4. Practice.

5. Production.

⟫→

2. Now write the stages of this teacher's lesson in the box.

'First we reviewed words for clothes, which the students had learnt last week, and then I taught them adjectives to describe materials (woollen, cotton, leather, etc.), and wrote them on the board. Then we looked at some pictures of people in the textbook, and they made sentences about them ("She's wearing a green cotton dress"). Then I asked them to write a few sentences about themselves, beginning "Last weekend I was wearing . . ." After that we read a text in the book about clothes people wear in different countries.'

1. ....

2. ....

3. ....

4. ....

5. ....

4   A lesson plan

Here is the lesson plan the teacher made for the second lesson in Activity 3. The teacher's notes accompanying the textbook only gave the most basic information, so he added several ideas of his own. Which parts do you think he added himself? How do they improve the lesson?

LESSON 16

Aim To practise talking about clothes, materials + colours.
New vocab. Adjectives: woollen, leather, cotton, nylon, plastic.
Structures Present continuous: ... is wearing... (revision).

1. Review Show pictures of clothes. Ss give words: coat, hat, shirt, trousers, etc.

2. Presentation Show objects made of wool, leather, plastic, etc. Present new adjectives. Write them on the board.

3. Practice 1) p.93 Ss look at pictures and make sentences e.g. 'She's wearing a green cotton dress'.
   2) Pairwork. A: What's she wearing?
                 B: She's wearing a green cotton dress.

---

4. <u>Writing</u> 1) Write on board : | 'Last week-end I was wearing...' |
Ss write sentences about themselves.
2) Collect about 10 students' papers. Read them out.
Others guess who wrote them!

5. <u>Reading</u> 1) Write on board : | Peru, Sudan, Pakistan | Ask: Where are they?
What's the climate like?
What do people wear there?
2) Ss read text p. 94 silently, and find answers to guiding questions.
3) Ask and answer questions p. 94.

5 Lesson preparation

1. Choose a lesson which you will teach soon, or find a lesson in a suitable textbook. If you have a teacher's book, look at the notes on the lesson. Do the notes tell you everything you need to do? Is there anything you could add to the lesson that is not in the notes, e.g.:

   your own examples   your own introduction to a text
   more practice   your own questions
   visual aids   review of previous lessons

2. Write a *lesson plan*. The plan should include:
   – the aim of the lesson;
   – new vocabulary or structures;
   – the main stages of activity;
   – detailed notes for each stage;
   – any visual aids you need.
   Use the lesson plan given in Activity 4 to help you.

Self-evaluation sheet

Complete this after you have taught the lesson.

1. What was the aim of the lesson?

2. What new structures or vocabulary did you teach?

3. Write down the main stages you actually followed in the lesson. About how long did each stage last?

Time

a)

b)

c)

d)

e)

Think about these questions.

Did the lesson plan help you? If so, in what way?
In what ways was your lesson different from the plan?

Think about each stage of the lesson.
Did you spend: too long? not long enough? the right amount of time?
How did you move from one stage to the next? What did you say to the class?

Think about the aims and the language you taught.
How many of the students *learned* what you set out to teach? How do you know?

9 Teaching basic reading

1 Learning to read

1. Here are some English words written in Newscript:

   school   2ᵧⅹ̄|

   class   ᵧ|ˢ2

   student   2|,ā̃scy|

   teacher |;ℙc⌐

   Here are the words in a different order. Can you recognise them?

   2|,ā̃scy|

   2ᵧⅹ̄|

   |;ℙc⌐

   ᵧ|ˢ2

Now cover the page down to this line.

2. Match the Newscript with the English words.

Newscript	English	
2ᵧⅹ̄|	student	....
ᵧ|ˢ2	teacher	....
|;ℙc⌐	class	....
2|,ā̃scy|	school	....

   Write the Newscript words in the correct place.

⟫→

3. Read this text.

In our town, there are only two ⌇ᵏᵃⁱ⌶ . This is not enough for so many people, so they are very crowded. In my ⌇ᵏᵃⁱ there are 1000 ⌇ᵃˢcⁱⁱⁱ, and only 25 ⌇ⱼᵏcⁱⱼ . There are 50 ⌇ᵃˢcⁱⁱⁱ in my ᵏⁱ⌶² . In some ᵏⁱ⌶²² there are even more.

4. Find these words in the text below.
   class   teacher   students

Now follow the text while the teacher reads. Then answer these questions.
   – How are *-ing* and *the* written in Newscript?
   – What is this letter? ႘

---

2   Look and say

Here is a technique for helping students to recognise words, using wordcards.

1. Hold up the first card ('a table'). Point to the card and say the words. Ask the class to repeat once.
   Do the same with the other cards.

2. Hold up the cards again, in a different
    order. This time, say nothing, and pause to
    give the whole class a chance to look at the
    word.

What is the advantage of using wordcards for this activity?

3   Simple reading tasks

Which word is different from the others?

a) doctor   nurse   hospital   ambulance   tractor
b) student   lion   elephant   monkey   bear
c) orange   rice   lemon   mango   banana
d) sleep   walk   jump   kick   run

Choose the correct sentence.

   a) He's kicking a ball.
   b) He's catching a ball.
   c) He's throwing a ball.

Do these things.

a) Point to the window.
b) Give a book to your friend.
c) Raise your left hand.
d) Put your finger to your lips.
e) Put your hands on your head.
f) Stand up, and then sit down again.

⟫→

Match the two halves of the sentences.

a) I ran to the station   because I was thirsty.
b) The postman knocked on my door   because my leg hurt terribly.
c) The doctor gave me an injection   because I was late.
d) I bought some lemonade   because there was a letter for me.

Choose *one* of these tasks. Design a similar activity, using words or structures that would suit your class.

4   Sounds and spelling

Look at these examples. What does each one show about English sounds and spelling? Think of more examples of each type.

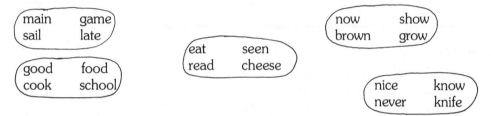

5   Lesson preparation

1. Prepare an activity which will focus on reading at an elementary level.
   Choose *one* of these:
   – simple word recognition practice using wordcards
   – a simple reading task
   – an activity focussing on sound/spelling relationships
   If there is a suitable activity in your textbook, use it or adapt it.
2. Plan the steps you would follow in the activity, and prepare any materials you would need.

Self-evaluation sheet *Complete this after you have taught the lesson.*

1. What activity did you use? Briefly describe it.

2. Write down the steps you followed.

    a)

    b)

    c)

    d)

Think about these questions.

What is the general level of the class? Can they:
– read only a few words with difficulty?
– understand simple sentences?
– read simple texts?

Was your activity above/at/below this level?

Think about individual students. Which students in your class:
– can read better than most?
– cannot read as well as most?
– cannot read at all?
What did these students do during the activity?
How did you help the weaker students?

How many students were actively involved in *reading*?
How many were just listening to the others or doing nothing?
What could you do to involve more of the class?

Did you use wordcards? If so, did you:
– hold them yourself?
– get students to hold them?
– stick them on the wall?
How well did this work?
Was the time spent preparing the cards worthwhile?

10   Teaching pronunciation

1   Introduction

Think about your students' pronunciation. What are their main problems?

Consonants	Vowels	Stress	Intonation

2   Focussing on a difficult sound

A. Imagine that you want to focus on a sound which students find difficult.
Which of these steps are most important? Which are not necessary?

Say the sound alone.	
Say the sound in a word.	
Contrast it with other sounds.	
Write words on the board.	
Explain how to make the sound.	
Get students to repeat the sound in chorus.	
Get individual students to repeat the sound.	

B. Work in groups.
    Teacher A: Choose a sound. Teach it to the others in your group. Help them
                   with any difficulties.
    The others: Imagine you are students. Make the same mistakes as your own
                   students would.

3   Practising sounds

Minimal pairs

1	2
will	well

Listen, and say the number: 1 or 2.

Missing words

Say a word to fill the gap.
a) A boy and a ....
b) First, second and ....
c) A pigeon is a kind of ....

Now listen to some more sentences, and say the missing words.

Making sentences

Make three sentences. In each sentence, use *one* word from
group 1 and *one* word from group 2.

Group 1
last   fast   calm
dark   black   glad
marvellous   bad

Group 2
farm   part   rabbit
party   jam   car
hat   man

Choose a sound that your students find difficult.
Make up an exercise like one of these to practise it.

4   Stress

1. Look at these words and phrases.
   – Which syllables are *stressed*? Mark them like this: disappointed
   – In the unstressed syllables, which vowels are *reduced*? Mark them like this:
     disappointed

disappointed	a kilo of sugar
attractive	give me an orange
trousers	I'd like some coffee
suppose	he was late again
perfect	we can leave as soon as you are ready

2. How could you show the stress pattern of a sentence in class:
   – using your voice?
   – using gestures?
   – using the blackboard?

5   Intonation

Look at these remarks. Which would normally have a *rising* intonation? Which would have a *falling* intonation?

A: I don't want anything to eat.
B: No?

A: Can I borrow some money?
B: No!

A: Who's that?
B: It's George.

A: Is that George?
B: No, it isn't.

How could you show intonation patterns in class?

6   Practising stress and intonation

Imagine that you want your class to repeat the sentences below.
– Practise saying the sentences.
– Mark the stressed syllables.
– Mark places where you could divide the sentences for 'back-chaining'.
– Mark rising or falling intonation.
(The first one is done for you.)

a) How long/have you/been/living here?

b) Have you ever been to London?

c) She's wearing a green dress.

d) What are you doing?

e) I haven't seen her for years.

f) Do you mind if I open the window?

g) You can sit down if you like.

7   Lesson preparation

1. Choose an aspect of pronunciation that your students (or other learners that
    you know) find difficult – it may be individual sounds, stress or intonation.
2. Plan part of a lesson focussing on the problem. Plan a short presentation
    followed by some practice.

Self-evaluation sheet   *Complete this after you have taught the lesson.*

1. Which pronunciation problem did you focus on in your lesson?

2. Write down the steps you followed in dealing with the problem.

   a)

   b)

   c)

   d)

   e)

Think about these questions.

How many of the class:
– have problems with pronunciation?
– had the particular problem you dealt with in your lesson?

Think of one student with *good* pronunciation.
What did you do to involve him or her in the activity?

Think of one student with *poor* pronunciation.
How much did he or she improve as a result of the activity?

How did the students react to the activity?
Do you think they felt it was: useful? interesting?
Why / Why not?

How much time did the activity take?
Was it more or less than you expected?
Was it too much time to spend on pronunciation? Or not enough?

Do you think you will do an activity like this again?
If so, what will you do differently next time?

Reference sheet: Weak vowels

The syllables in italics are all unstressed, and are pronounced /ə/ or /ɪ/.

A. Words with /ə/
Occupations: teach*er*, driv*er*, paint*er*, doct*or*, act*or*, sail*or*.
Comparatives: bett*er*, long*er*, bigg*er*, larg*er*.
Beginning 'a-': *a*bout, *a*go, *a*sleep, *a*long, *a*round.
Ending '-ory', '-ary': fact*ory*, libr*ary*, hist*ory*, tempor*ary*.
Ending '-ion', '-ian': nat*ion*, Egypt*ian*, informat*ion*, Russ*ian*.
Ending '-man': wom*an*, policem*an*, Englishm*an*, countrym*an*.
Others: sug*ar*, isl*an*d, seas*on*, pers*on*, less*on*, bott*om*, breakf*a*st, sec*on*d, centr*al*, chocol*a*te, par*en*t, happ*en*, pleas*an*t.

B. Words with /ɪ/
Days: Sund*ay*, Mond*ay*, Tuesd*ay*, etc.
Numbers: Twent*y*, thirt*y*, fort*y*, etc.
Plurals: hors*es*, match*es*, glass*es*, box*es*, etc.
Third person endings: wash*es*, finish*es*, miss*es*, dress*es*, etc.
Past forms: marri*ed*, hurri*ed*, visit*ed*, wait*ed*, etc.
Superlatives: long*est*, short*est*, bigg*est*, fast*est*, etc.
Ending '-age', '-ege': lugg*age*, marr*iage*, langu*age*, coll*ege*.
Beginning 'be-', 're-': *be*gin, *be*have, *be*fore, *be*cause, *re*ligion, *re*main, *re*ply, *re*member.
Others: mark*et*, pack*et*, or*a*nge, chick*en*, kitch*en*, wom*en*.

Background text: Structures and functions

The ultimate aim of all English teaching is for students to 'know English', or at least know enough English for whatever purpose they have in learning the language. In this text we shall consider what 'knowing English' entails – in other words, what are the aspects of the language that need to be learnt?

This question appears to be fairly straightforward. Clearly, students need to develop skills, e.g. speaking, listening, reading and writing; how much attention is paid to each skill will depend on the students' needs and interests.

Within the productive skills (speaking and writing), we can say that students need to learn words and phrases to *express* meanings in English; they also need to be able to produce basic structures correctly. In speaking, this will involve learning the sound system and stress and intonation patterns; in writing, it will involve learning features of the writing system, such as spelling and punctuation. Since we do not speak or write in isolated sentences, they will also need to learn ways of joining sentences together in connected speech or writing.

Within the receptive skills (listening and reading), we can say that students need to *understand* words and structures in their spoken and written forms, and also understand the connecting devices that link them together. (All of this says nothing, of course, about *how* students learn, and does not necessarily mean that all these items need to be individually taught.)

A student who has learnt all these things, then, would be able to understand connected speech and writing and produce correct sentences in English. But this does not quite amount to 'knowing English'; for language is not merely an abstract system which is used for making correct sentences; it is a way of communicating with other people. 'Knowing English', therefore, must mean knowing how to communicate in English. This involves not only producing language correctly, but using language for particular purposes; for example, being able to give advice in English, make predictions, describe people. We call these the *functions* (or 'communicative functions') of language.

Here are some examples of common English structures and the functions they express:

Structures	*Functions*
There's a hotel in the town centre.	Describing
I'm going to study engineering.	Expressing intention
I wish I'd left earlier.	Expressing regret
The population *is likely to* increase.	Making a prediction
You *can* go home now.	Giving permission

(Note that one communicative function can be expressed by a range of different structures, e.g. intention can be expressed by 'I'm going to', 'I'm planning to', 'I intend to', etc.)

50

If learners are able not only to produce and understand structures like those in the examples, but also use them to express the communicative functions they need, that is, to do things through language, we say that they have 'communicative competence' in the language.

How does this affect language learning and teaching? Obviously, students do not need to 'learn' functions, since they are universal to all languages; but they do need to learn how to express these functions in English. Recognising the importance of functions will give the lesson a different emphasis, and students will be more aware of *why* they are practising particular structures. For example, in a class where the teacher is aware of functions as well as structures, students will not learn 'there is/are' for its own sake or because it is a 'useful structure'. Rather, they will learn *how to describe places*, and in doing so will practise 'there is/are', as well as other necessary structures (e.g. place prepositions). Rather than doing a series of exercises which practise 'going to' for no obvious reason, students will practise using this structure for a recognisable communicative purpose: for example, to talk about their own intentions and plans.

This same difference of emphasis is shown in the comments of the three teachers in Unit 8 Activity 2. Teacher B is concerned with teaching a useful structure; Teacher C is aware not only of the structure but also of the function the structure is used for. Of the two lessons, Teacher C's is likely to have a much clearer purpose.

Discussion

1. Look at the exercises in these activities:
   – Unit 6 Activities 1 and 2
   – Unit 7 Activity 3B
   – Unit 13 Activity 1
   What functions are the structures used for?
2. Look at a lesson in your textbook or a suitable textbook. What are the main structures taught? What communicative function do the structures express?
3. Look at the Contents page in your textbook. Do the descriptions of each unit emphasise the structures taught or the functions?

11　Teaching handwriting

1　What style to teach?

Thank you for your letter of 14th

thank you for your letter of 14th

Thank you for your letter of 14th

How are these three styles different?
Which one do you think is:
− easiest to learn?
− most useful?

2　Teaching a new letter

Imagine you are teaching a new letter. Which of these steps are important?
Which are not important?

Draw lines on the board.	
Write the letter clearly on the board.	
Describe how the letter is formed.	
Say the name of the letter.	
Give the sound of the letter.	
Students repeat the name of the letter.	
Students repeat the sound.	
Students draw the letter in the air.	
Students copy the letter in their books.	

... round, up, and back down again ...

3   Practice

Work in groups.
Teacher A: Choose a letter. Teach it to the others in your group. Help them with
any difficulties.
The others: Imagine you are students. Practise writing the new letter. Make the
same mistakes as your own students would.

4   Simple copying tasks

A.

Match the questions with the answers, then write them out.

What's the time?   Yes, I love them.
Do you like oranges?   At half past seven.
When do you get up?   No, I go by bus.
Do you walk to school ?   It's two o' clock.

B.

Copy the *true* sentences only.

This man is wearing a hat.
He's carrying a stick.
He's running.
He's smiling.

C.

Some of these are *farm animals*, others are *wild animals*. Write
them in two lists.

	Farm animals	Wild animals
goat tiger horse buffalo lion bear chicken cow camel	horse	lion

5   Handwriting problems

However, the tress are disappearing
By 1974, a quarter of the forest had already
been cut down.

However, The Trees are disappearing. By 1974,
a quarter of The Forest had already been cut
down.

What handwriting problems do these students seem to have?

Choose one of the problems. Plan a short piece of teaching to focus on the problem.

6   Lesson preparation

1. Collect examples of your own students' handwriting or samples of writing from other learners. Choose one problem that most of the students seem to have.
2. Plan part of a lesson in which you would focus on the problem. Prepare a short presentation followed by some practice.

Self-evaluation sheet   *Complete this after you have taught the lesson.*

1. Which handwriting problem did you focus on in your lesson?

2. Write down the steps you followed in dealing with the problem.

   a)

   b)

   c)

   d)

   e)

Think about these questions.

Was the activity useful for: all the class? most of the class? some of the class?
Was it easy or difficult for most students?
Think of one good student and one weak student. What did each of them do?

How much time did the activity take?
Was it more/less than you expected?
Was it too much time to spend on handwriting? Or not enough?

Was your teaching successful?
Did the students understand the point you were teaching?
What improvement did you notice in their writing?

Think of a similar activity for a future lesson.
When would you focus on handwriting again?
What would you do next time?

Reference sheet: Letter formation

Small letters

This shows:
- the small letters divided into 'shape groups' (letters in each group have the same basic shape);
- basic shapes, which students can practise before they learn the letters in the group;
- how the letters are formed (indicated by the arrows).

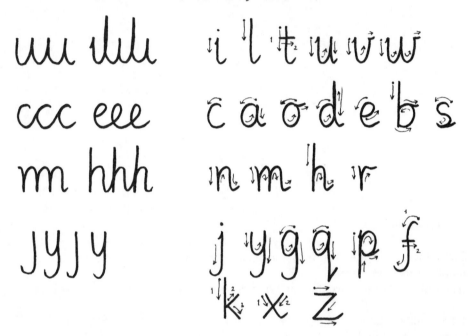

Capital letters

Capital letters are shown here in alphabetical order, but could be taught at the same time as the corresponding small letter.

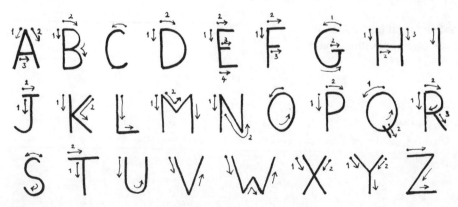

12 Pairwork and groupwork

1 Pair and group activities

A. Work in pairs. Ask and answer the questions.
What happens if . . .
a) you eat unripe fruit?
b) you eat too much food?
c) you leave ice in the sun?
d) you drive over broken glass?
e) you drop a match into a can of petrol?
f) you sit in the sun too long?
g) you leave milk for a few days?

Now think of two more questions like this.

B. Work in pairs.
1. Can you answer these questions?
   – What is acid rain?
   – How is it caused?
   – What damage does it do?
2. Read the text and find the answers.
3. Underline all the words in the text which you do not understand.
   With your partner, try to guess what they mean.

Throughout Europe, and also in other areas of the world such as India, China and parts of America, forests are being destroyed. According to one prediction, 90% of Germany's forests will have vanished by the end of the century. This destruction is caused by air pollution. Power stations and cars are mainly responsible – they emit gases into the air which, after a series of chemical changes, turn into toxic acids. These acids fall as 'acid rain', raising the level of acidity in the soil, in lakes and in rivers to dangerous levels, and destroying not only trees but also fish and other wildlife. The industrialised world is slowly waking up to the fact that urgent action is needed to reduce air pollution, otherwise our environment will be damaged beyond repair.

⋙→

C. Work in groups.

nurse	farm worker
doctor	taxi driver
teacher	engineer

1. Which of these people earns the most money in your country? Write them in a list, starting with the highest paid and ending with the lowest paid.
2. Who do you think should earn the most money? Who should earn more, and who should earn less?

2   Advantages and problems

What are the *advantages* of using pairwork and groupwork?
What *problems* might there be?

Advantages	Problems

How could you overcome the problems?

3   Organising pairwork

Teacher X had an intermediate class. She presented 'like / don't like', and then she used this exercise for freer practice in pairs:

Exercise 3 Likes and dislikes

**Pairwork. Ask what your friend likes and doesn't like.
Ask about:**
   food   sport   music   school subjects

The pictures below show what she did before, during and after the activity.

Before: *During:*   *After:*

Do you think the activity was successful?
What do you think might have gone wrong?
What could she do to make it more successful?

4   Dividing the class

1. Here are two rows of a class of 50 students. The desks are fixed, and the students sit on chairs. How could you divide the class into:
   – pairs?
   – small groups?
   What instructions would you give?

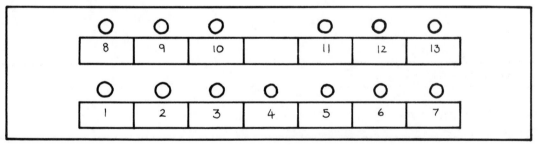

2. Draw a plan of your own class. Show how you would divide the class for a pairwork or a groupwork activity.

5   Activities in class

1. Which of these activities do you often do in your own class?
   pattern practice
   practising short dialogues
   reading a text and answering questions
   short writing exercises
   discussions
   grammar exercises
2. Discuss each activity.
   – Could you use pairwork or groupwork for part of the activity?
   – If so, exactly what would students do in pairs or groups?
   – What would you need to do before the pair/groupwork stage?
     Is there anything you would do *after* it?

6   Lesson preparation

1. Look at a lesson which you will teach soon, or find a lesson in a suitable
   textbook. Choose an activity (or part of an activity) which would be suitable for
   pairwork or groupwork.
2. Plan that part of the lesson.
   – Decide how to divide the class into pairs or groups. (Use the plan you drew
     in Activity 4.)
   – Plan an introduction or demonstration, to make it clear to the class what
     they have to do.
   – Plan a short 'round-up' stage to follow the pair/group activity.

Self-evaluation sheet

Complete this after you have taught the lesson.

1. What was the activity?
   Did you organise the class in pairs or in groups?

2. What skills did students practise: speaking? writing? reading? listening?

3. Write down the main steps you followed in the activity.

a)

b)

c)

d)

e)

Think about these questions.

How did students respond to working in pairs/groups?
Did they find it: enjoyable? useful? difficult?

How long did the activity last?
Did it last a longer or a shorter time than you expected?

What did you do while the pair/group activity was going on?
Did you:
– listen to students?
– watch students?
– help students who were confused?
– correct students' mistakes?
– take part in the activity?
Which of these was the most useful? Which was the least useful?

Did you find it difficult to:
– divide students into pairs/groups?
– get the activity started?
– control the activity?
– stop the activity?
How did you overcome these difficulties?
How might you overcome them next time?

Look again at the list of advantages and problems on page 58.
Has your opinion about any of them changed as a result of your lesson?

13   Writing activities

1   Controlled writing

A.

> *Gap-filling* Listen to the teacher, then write out the complete sentences.
>
> Paper .... wood. It .... the
> Chinese in ....

B.

> *Re-ordering words* Write the sentences correctly.
>
> We/six o'clock/and/tea/drink/get up/at.
> Then/the patients/wake/go/and/the wards/we/round.
> Sometimes/medicines/injections/them/we/or/give.

C.

> *Substitution* Write a true sentence like this about yourself.
>
> Samir enjoys playing football and reading adventure stories.

D.

> *Correct the facts* Re-write the sentences so that they match the picture.
>
> At the market, I saw an old woman sitting in a chair. She was selling eggs. It was raining.

2   Writing based on a text

Jopley is a small town in the north of England. It is on the River Ouse, not far from Leeds. The town has a wide main street, with a stone church, the town hall and a cinema. There is a large supermarket in the town centre, and many smaller shops and cafés. Most people in Jopley work in the local factory, which produces farm machinery.

1. Write a similar paragraph about Bexham. Use these notes:
   Bexham – small village – south coast.
   Narrow street – two shops – church.
   Most people – farmers. Grow vegetables, wheat.

2. Now write about your own town or village.

Adapt this exercise so that it is about your own country.
Then discuss:
– What difficulty might your students have in writing the paragraph?
– What preparation could you do to make the activity easier?

3   Oral preparation

1. This teacher is building up notes on the board for a description of Cairo, in Egypt.

What were the teacher's first three questions?
What will he write next?

2. The teacher wants to elicit these other facts about Cairo, and write them on the board.

    What questions could he ask?

> *Important business centre*
> *– international hotels*
> *Tourists:*
> *– The Pyramids (2500 BC)*
> *– many famous mosques*
> *– market area (gold, copper, leather)*
> *Very crowded-traffic problems*
> *– new underground railway*

4   Correcting written work

Here are four teachers' techniques for correcting written work.

Teacher A:

> I collect the books at the end of the lesson, and correct them during the lunch hour. Then I give the books back the next day.

Teacher B:

> I just go through the answers and get students to correct their own work. Sometimes I write sentences on the board.

Teacher C:

> I ask the students to sit in pairs and correct each other's work, helping each other. Then we all go through the answers together.

Teacher D:

> I ask students to exchange books with the person next to them. Then I go through the answers and they correct each other's work.

Which of these techniques would succeed in your class?

5   Lesson preparation

1. Prepare a short writing activity for a lesson. Use any of the techniques introduced in this unit. If there is a suitable activity in the textbook, use it or adapt it. The activity should develop *writing skills*, not just practise grammar.
2. Plan carefully:
    – any material you need for the activity (e.g. texts, pictures);
    – anything you would write on the blackboard;
    – any oral preparation you would need to do before the activity.

Self-evaluation sheet

Complete this after you have taught the lesson.

1. What kind of writing activity did you do? Briefly describe it.

2. Write down the main stages of the activity.

   a)

   b)

   c)

   d)

Think about these questions.

Did you use an activity in the textbook? If so:
– How successful was it?
– Could you have changed it or improved it in any way?

Did you adapt an activity from the textbook? If so:
– How successful was your adaptation?
– Would you make any other changes next time?

Did you use an activity of your own? If so:
– How well did it work?
– How could you improve it next time?

How long did the activity take?
How much time was spent on: oral preparation/discussion? writing? follow-up/correction?

Do you think the time spent on writing was too long? about right? not long enough?

Was it a good idea to do the activity in class (rather than for homework)?
What advantages were there? Were there any disadvantages?

Did most students find the writing task easy or difficult?
Were any students unable to complete the task?
If so, did you help them? How?

Did any students finish before the others?
How did you keep them involved?

What mistakes did students make? How serious were they?
Did you correct them? How successful were your corrections?

14 Eliciting

1 Eliciting from pictures

A.

A teacher uses this picture to elicit vocabulary. Below are the answers she wants the students to give. What questions should she ask?

T: .... ?
Ss: Farmers. They're returning from the fields.
T: .... ?
Ss: Donkeys. A buffalo.
T: .... ?
Ss: He's riding the donkey.
T: .... ?
Ss: It's evening. End of the day.
T: .... ?
Ss: Because the sun is low. It's setting.
T: .... ?
Ss: They're going home.

B.

You are using this picture to elicit the words
in the box. What questions could you ask?
What other words could you elicit from the
picture?

> rice
> to plant
> by hand
> bend down
> rows

2   Getting students to guess

What do these examples show?
Can you think of more examples of the same type?
Write them down.

> Egypt – Egyptian
> Russia – Russian
> Brazil – Brazilian

> buy – bought
> catch – caught
> think – thought

> leaf – leaves
> loaf – loaves

> interesting – more interesting
> beautiful – more beautiful

> sleep – slept
> meet – met
> feel – felt

> short – shorter
> big – bigger

> date late make
> play say day
> wait sail pain

3   Getting students to imagine

A. Look at the picture and answer the questions.

Where is this woman standing?

What is she wearing?

What is she doing?

What is she holding in her hand?

What time of day is it?

Why is she standing here? What has happened?

How does she feel? Why?

What is she thinking? Write some of her thoughts in a few words.

Imagine this is a scene from a film. What will happen next?

How are the questions on the left of the picture different from those on the right?

B. Think of three interesting questions to ask about the picture below. The questions should encourage students to *interpret* the picture or to *imagine* something. Write your questions down.

C. Think of similar questions to ask about the pictures in Activity 1.

4   **Lesson preparation**

1. Choose a lesson which you will teach soon, or find a lesson in a suitable
   textbook. Focus on parts of the lesson where you would normally present new
   language or introduce a topic. Choose five items that you could try to *elicit*
   from the class instead of simply presenting them.
   Plan exactly how you would elicit these items. Write down the questions you
   would ask.
2. Are there any pictures, texts or dialogues in the lesson?
   If so, write three questions you could ask about them which would require
   students to interpret or to use their imagination.

Self-evaluation sheet   *Complete this after you have taught the lesson.*

1. What words or structures did you try to elicit? Write them down.

   a)

   b)

   c)

   d)

   e)

   Write either **E** or **P** against each one. (**E** = you managed to *elicit* the item (a student gave the word or structure correctly); **P** = no-one knew the item, so you *presented* it.)
   Were you able to elicit more or less than you expected?

2. Write down the three questions you asked which required students to interpret or imagine.

   a)

   b)

   c)

   What *answers* did students give?
   How many students answered?

Think about these questions.

How did the class react when you elicited words?
Did they seem: eager to answer? involved? shy? confused?

Was it at all difficult to:
– control the class?
– lead students towards the answer you wanted?
– involve weaker students?
How could you overcome these difficulties?

15 Reading activities

---

1 Pre-reading activities

Work in groups. Do *one* of these activities *before* you read the text.

A.

> You are going to read a text about the earthquake in the picture.
> What would you like to know about the earthquake? Write
> down at least *five* questions, which you hope the text will answer.

⟫→

B.

> You are going to read a text about the earthquake in the picture.
> Try to *imagine* what the text will tell you about:
>   buildings
>   boats
>   people
>   hills around the city
>   trains
>   the land and the sea

C.

> You are going to read a text about the earthquake in the picture.
> Here are some words and phrases from the text. Can you guess
> how they are used in the text?
>   the sea-bed   the Richter scale   a huge wave
>   tremors   massive shocks   having a bath
>   Tokyo and Yokohama

Now read the text.

> At two minutes to noon on 1 September 1923, the great clock in
> Tokyo stopped. Tokyo Bay shook as if a huge rug had been
> pulled from under it. Towering above the bay, the 4,000 metre
> Mount Fuji stood above a deep trench in the sea. It was from this
> trench that the earthquake came, at a magnitude of 8.3 on the
> Richter scale.
>
> The sea drew back for a few moments. Then, a huge wave
> swept over the city. Boats were carried inland, and buildings and
> people were dragged out to sea. The tremors dislodged part of a
> hillside, which gave way, brushing trains, stations and bodies
> into the water below. Large sections of the sea-bed sank
> 400 metres; the land rose by 250 metres in some places and sank
> in others. Three massive shocks wrecked the cities of Tokyo and
> Yokohama and, during the next six hours, there were 171
> aftershocks.
>
> The casualties were enormous, but there were also some lucky
> survivors. The most remarkable was a woman who was having a
> bath in her room at the Tokyo Grand Hotel. As the hotel
> collapsed, she and her bath gracefully descended to the street,
> leaving both her and the bathwater intact.

(from *Earthquakes and Volcanoes*: S. Steel)

2   Using questions on a text

Here are some of the questions which followed the text.

> 1. What time did the earthquake start?
>   What time did it finish?
>
> 2. Did it start: a) in the mountains?
>   b) in the sea?
>   c) in the city?
>
> 3. Beside each sentence, write T(= true), F(= false) or D/K
>   (= we don't know from the text).
> a) Parts of the sea became deeper.
> b) A hillside slid down onto the city.
> c) Most people died by drowning.
> d) The Grand Hotel survived the earthquake.
> e) The woman in the bath survived the earthquake.

Three teachers used the questions in different ways.

Teacher A:

My students sat in groups
to answer the questions.
Then we went through
 the answers together.

Teacher B:

I asked my students to write
the answers to the questions.
Then we went through the
 answers together.

Teacher C:

I asked the questions round
the class, and got different
 students to answer.

Which approach do you think is the most effective? Why?

3   Completing a table

Read the text and complete the table below.

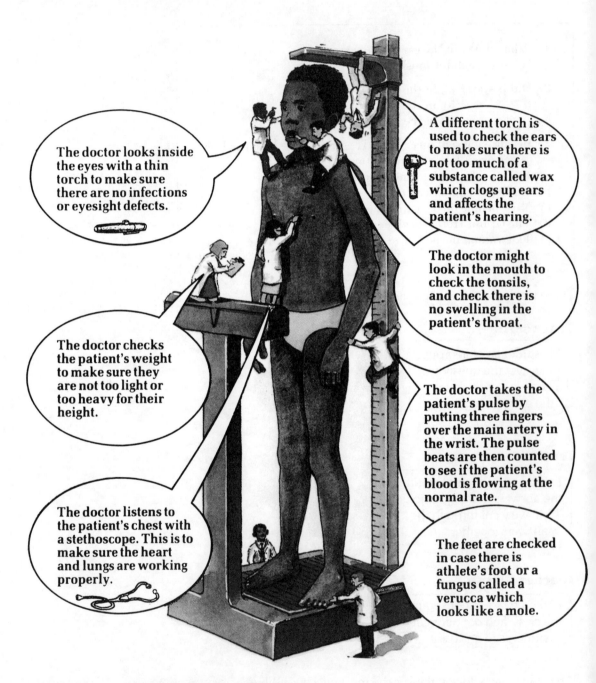

The doctor looks inside the eyes with a thin torch to make sure there are no infections or eyesight defects.

A different torch is used to check the ears to make sure there is not too much of a substance called wax which clogs up ears and affects the patient's hearing.

The doctor might look in the mouth to check the tonsils, and check there is no swelling in the patient's throat.

The doctor checks the patient's weight to make sure they are not too light or too heavy for their height.

The doctor takes the patient's pulse by putting three fingers over the main artery in the wrist. The pulse beats are then counted to see if the patient's blood is flowing at the normal rate.

The doctor listens to the patient's chest with a stethoscope. This is to make sure the heart and lungs are working properly.

The feet are checked in case there is athlete's foot or a fungus called a verucca which looks like a mole.

(from *The Young Scientist Book of Medicine*: P. Beasant)

THE DOCTOR

examines:	uses:	wants to know:
a) eyes	torch	i) any infections? ii) eyesight ok?
b) weight		
c)		
d)		
e)		
f)		
g)		

4   Responding to a text

Work in groups. Read this text and answer the questions.

When you are invited to a meal in Thailand, the words of the invitation literally mean 'come and eat rice'. Indeed, nearly all Thai dishes are eaten with rice, which grows there very easily as the climate is warm and there is plenty of rain.

The food is always served in neatly cut up pieces, so there is no need to use knives and forks but, instead, special spoons and forks are used. The Thais used to eat with their hands and there are still some people who eat this way. There is a particular way of doing it. First they wash their right hand in a bowl of water – they only eat with their right hand. They are careful not to let the food touch the palm of their hand. After the meal, the hand is again carefully washed.

The meal is usually made up of several different dishes, all of which are spicy. They are served in bowls which everyone shares, though each person has their own bowl of rice. As Thailand has a long coastline, it not surprising that fish and shellfish play an important part in Thai cooking.

(from *What the World Eats*: T. and J. Watson)

⟫→

A. 1. Why is rice a common food in Thailand?
    2. Why is fish a common food?
    3. Why are knives not needed to eat food?
    4. Here are some statements about the traditional way of eating in Thailand.
        Which are *true*, and which are *false*?
        a) You should wash both hands before eating in Thailand.
        b) You should eat with the fingers of the right hand.
        c) You should wash your right hand after eating.

B. 1. Write two lists:
        – Things that are *the same* in Thailand as in your own country.
        – Things that are *different* in Thailand from your own country.
    2. Imagine you are eating with a Thai family. What would you find *most*
        unusual. Why?
    3. Do you think you would enjoy Thai food? Why? / Why not?

Compare the questions in A and those in B. What is the difference between
them?

5   Lesson preparation

1. Choose a text which you will be using soon, or find a suitable text. Look at it
    carefully.
    Are there any activities before the text?
    How good are the questions? Do they help students to read the text?
    Do any questions go beyond the text? Are there any 'reading tasks'?
2. Plan *one or more* of these activities:
    – a pre-reading activity
    – a table for students to complete
    – a few questions which require a personal response from the students

Self-evaluation sheet

Complete this after you have taught the lesson.

1. What were the main stages of your lesson? Write them down.

   a)

   b)

   c)

   d)

   e)

   f)

2. At which stages of the lesson (if at all) did you depart from the textbook and use ideas of your own? Mark them above, like this: ★

Think about these questions.

Think about the parts of the lesson marked ★.
Did they improve the lesson? If so, how?
If you could teach these parts of the lesson again, what changes would you make?

How did the students react to the text?
Did they find it: interesting? boring? difficult? easy?
Think of the three *weakest* students in the class.
Could they understand the text? What did you do to help them?

Did students answer questions on the text? If so:
– Did they answer: orally round the class? in groups? by writing the answers?
– In general, how well did the questions help students to understand the text?
– Were any questions: too easy? too difficult? impossible to answer?

Did any questions require personal responses from the students? If so:
– What were the questions?
– What different replies did students give?

Did students complete a table? If so:
– How many students completed it successfully?
– Were there any problems in: organising the task? going through the answers?
How did you overcome them?

Background text: Learning a language

We cannot easily evaluate teaching methods without some idea of how students learn. Exactly how we learn our own or a second language is still not completely certain, but we do know in general terms what is involved in the process of language learning. In this text we shall look briefly at three different kinds of learning, and consider their importance in learning a language: *learning by heart*, *forming habits*, and *acquiring rules*.

Learning by heart

A traditional approach to learning is learning by heart, and many people still attempt to learn languages by learning set sentences, dialogues, and texts by heart. Learning by heart is likely to be most useful in learning things which are fixed and limited, and it is often found to be a useful way of mastering certain fixed items in a language, such as numerals or irregular past tense forms. The problem with learning by heart as a strategy for learning the whole of a language is that language is not something which is limited and finite; using a language involves understanding and producing an infinite variety of sentences. For example, we could easily learn the following dialogue by heart:
– Do you have any children?
– Yes, a boy and two girls.
We could then say that we have 'learnt' a small sample of English. But this in itself would be of little use to us; for to speak English we may need to make any one of hundreds of questions with 'Do you . . .?', and to use the word 'children' in hundreds of quite different sentences. Learning set sentences by heart may enable us to give a few fixed responses, but it is not likely to prepare us for this great variety of language that we need to understand and use. It seems clear that language is not something that we can 'learn' in the same way that we might learn a poem or a set of instructions; it is not a body of knowledge but a set of skills, so 'learning a language' must mean learning to use those skills.

Forming habits

Another view of how language is learnt is to see it as developing a set of 'habits' which we learn by imitation and which gradually become automatic; in this view, language is seen as similar to more mechanical activities such as eating or swimming. Central to this view is the belief that children learn their first language by imitating their parents and by reinforcement on the part of the parents (the parents 'reward' correct sentences by responding positively to them). This view of language learning is associated with the behaviourist school of psychology and is reflected in the audio-lingual approach to language teaching, which was popular in the 1950s and 1960s. Applied to learning a second language, it emphasises the importance of repetition and drilling; and as language is thought to be learnt by repeating correct sentences, it is considered important for students to avoid making errors.

Two main arguments have been put forward against this view of language learning. The first argument is concerned with the creative nature of language, which we illustrated in the preceding section; in using language we are continually required to produce completely new sentences which we may never have used or even heard before, and it is difficult to see how we could do this if learning depended entirely on imitation and reinforcement. The second argument is based on research into the way children learn their first language. Research has suggested that children do not learn their first language only, or even mainly, by imitation; they frequently produce sentences which they could never have heard from adults, and so must have developed independently. A simple example of this is children's use of plural nouns: when English-speaking children first begin to use plurals, they often say phrases such as 'two mans', 'three sheeps'. It is clear that they have not learnt to produce these by imitation; rather it appears that they have acquired a *rule* of the language, which at this stage they are applying to all plural nouns.

Acquiring rules

This suggests a third view of the language learning process, which sees language as a system of rules. Learning a language involves being exposed to samples of language that we can understand; from this we can acquire the rules of the language and apply them to make an unlimited number of original sentences. During the process of learning either our first language or a second language, the rules we apply will often be incomplete or slightly different from the actual rules of the language, and this will lead to errors. In this view, therefore, errors are a natural part of the acquisition process, and need not be completely avoided.

It is important to clarify what we mean by 'acquiring the rules' of a language. It means being able to *apply* the rules (in other words, to understand and use the language correctly); it does not necessarily mean knowing how to *explain* the rules (in other words, to talk about the language). All native speakers of English 'know' the difference between the present perfect and past tenses, in the sense that they use them correctly, but very few would be able to explain the difference; by contrast, some learners of English can explain the difference between the two tenses (they 'know' the rule) but they cannot use the tenses correctly. It is, of course, applying the rules that is important in language learning; and in the case of our first language this is an entirely subconscious process. It may be that in learning a second language too the best way to acquire rules is subconsciously, by reading and listening to language we understand and by attempting to communicate in the language, rather than by consciously 'learning grammar'.

We have considered three views of the learning process: learning by heart, forming habits by drilling and repetition, and acquiring rules naturally through attempts to communicate. All these are valid views of the ways in which language skills can be developed although the third is the most powerful. Demonstration and habit formation undoubtedly have a role to play but if our aim is to develop the skill to communicate in unpredicted circumstances then we have to provide our learners with the opportunity to acquire the underlying rules of the language themselves.

Discussion

Following the ideas in this text, what conclusions might you come to about:
1. students' errors
2. repetition drills
3. explaining grammar rules
4. using English in class

16 Correcting errors

1 Introduction

Here are three teachers' approaches to correcting errors.

Teacher A:

> I never let my students make mistakes. If they say anything wrong, I stop them and make them say it correctly. I don't want them to learn bad English from each other.

Teacher B:

> I correct students sometimes, but not all the time. If we're practising one particular language point, then I insist that they say it correctly. But if we're doing a freer activity then I try not to correct too much. If I do correct students, I try to do it in an encouraging way.

Teacher C:

> I try to correct errors as little as possible. I want my students to express themselves in English without worrying too much about making mistakes. Sometimes I notice points that everyone gets wrong, and deal with them later – but I never interrupt students to correct them.

Think of yourself as a *learner*. Which teacher would you prefer? Why?

2   Strategies for correcting errors

Here is part of a letter, written by a student called Carlos to his pen-friend Marco.

You read this text with the class in an earlier lesson. Now you are asking questions to review the main words and structures.

> Dear Marco,
>   I was very glad to get your letter and to hear about all the things you are doing.
>   Thank you for sending the stamps. They are very beautiful and I have added them to my collection.
>   I am sending you a few photographs of my family. The tall girl with dark hair is my elder sister, and the shorter one is my cousin. I

You ask the question: 'What does Carlos do?'
What would you do if:
a) A student answers: 'Carlos collects the stamps'.
b) A student answers: 'He collects'.
c) A student cannot answer at all.
d) One of the *weakest* students answers: 'He collecting stamps'.
e) One of the *best* students answers: 'He collecting stamps'.
f) A student answers: 'He writes a letter'.

3   Helping students to correct themselves

1.

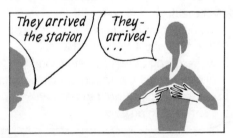

2. Here are some sentences spoken by students. What is the error in each one? What *gestures* could you use to help the students correct the errors themselves?

Work in pairs. Act out each 'dialogue' between the teacher and the student.

4   Correcting written work

Here is some written work, corrected by a teacher.

Machiko

> I think the most important sense is hearing.
> If I lose the ability of hearing, I ~~also can't speak.~~ *cannot speak either.*
>   [TO HEAR] *one's*   *LOSING*   *human faculties*
> To lose hearing means ~~to lose~~ two important functions ~~of human~~. *s*
>
>   Deaf-and-dumb people cannot hear ~~the~~ noise
>   *behind them*
> even if ~~the~~ accident happens ~~in their back~~. This is
>   *an*
> (problem) the most important ploblem for them. For example,
>   *R*   *are riding*
> suppose that they ride a bike in ~~the~~ busy street.
>   *a*
>   *sense*
> We, normal people ~~feel~~ the danger~~ous~~ by the noise
> (Lorry lorries) which is made by cars and lorrys. *ie* *Because we can hear...* As a result of
> hearing the noise, we can avoide them??? and
>   *ride*
> (drive) safely. Deaf-and-dumb people ~~always~~
> ~~expose their to danger~~. ... *are always exposed to danger.*

1. How could the teacher's corrections be made:
    – clearer?
    – less discouraging?
    – more useful to the student?
2. Now correct the student's work yourself.

> I think the most important sense is hearing.
> If I lose the ability of hearing, I also can't speak.
> To lose hearing means to lose two important function of
> human.
>   Deaf-and-dumb people cannot hear the noise
> even if the accident happens in their back. This is
> the most important ploblem for them. For example,
> suppose that they ride a bike in the busy street.
> We, normal people feel the dangerous by the noise
> which is made by cars and lorrys. As a result of
> hearing the noise, we can avoide them and
> drive safely. Deaf-and-dumb people always
> expose their to danger.

5   Common written errors

Work in groups.
Look at examples of common errors which your own students have made.
Choose *five* which you think are important, and discuss:
– What seems to be the cause of each error?
– Does it show something the students do not understand? Or is it something
  they understand but still get wrong?
– What should you do about it?

6   Lesson preparation

1. Either choose *one* of the errors which you discussed in Activity 5 or one other
   error which your students (or other learners that you know) frequently make.
2. Plan part of a lesson in which you would focus on this error. Plan a short
   presentation followed by some practice.

Self-evaluation sheet

Complete this after you have taught the lesson.

1. Which error did you deal with?

2. What do you think was the cause of the error?

3. What steps did you follow in dealing with it? Write them down.

a)

b)

c)

d)

e)

Think about these questions.

How many students in the class made this error?
How many do you think really didn't understand the correct form?

When you presented the correct form again, how many seemed to understand?

Did you give students a chance to practise the correct form?
How many could do the practice successfully?

Think of one good student and one weaker student in your class.
What exactly did they do:
– during your presentation?
– during the practice?

Do you think your students will now stop making this error?
If they continue to make it, what will you do?

17   Listening activities

1   Focussed listening

A. The trainer will talk to you about himself/herself.
   Listen and write notes in the table.

Home town	
Brothers/sisters	
Children	
Interests	
Holidays	

B. You will hear a text about someone's childhood. Listen and try to answer these questions.

1. Where did he stay?
2. What does he say about:
   - the river?
   - his bicycle?
   - the fruit trees?

2   Helping students to listen

A teacher used this dialogue for listening. Below, she describes what she did and how well it worked.

Doctor: Now then, what seems to be the matter?
Peter: Well, I've got a sore throat. I've had it for three days now. It's really sore – it hurts when I try to swallow, and it's very painful if I try to eat anything hard, like bread or anything like that. And I feel a bit cold and shivery all the time.
Doctor: Open your mouth and let's have a look.

. . . .

Well, you've got a throat infection, but it's nothing serious. Here you are – take this to the chemist's and he'll give you some tablets to take. That should clear it up. If it isn't better in two or three days, come and see me again.

1. Which sentences are *true*, which are *false*?
   a) Peter has a sore throat.
   b) He feels hot.
   c) He can't eat bread.

I told the class to close their books and listen, and I read the dialogue twice. Then I asked the questions. But they couldn't answer most of them. So I told them to open their books, and we read the dialogue together. Then they seemed to find it quite easy. They couldn't understand it from just listening – it was too difficult for them.

What could the teacher do to *help* the students to listen?

3   Using the cassette recorder

Imagine you are using the dialogue in Activity 2 for intensive listening, using a cassette recorder.
Which parts of the text would you focus the students' attention on?
Underline them, and mark places where you would pause the recording.

4   Getting students to predict

A. Work in pairs. Read this story.

> Once there was a boy called Ali, a poor fisherman's son. As he was going home one evening, he saw an old man lying by the side of the road, seriously ill. The boy was very kind, and he helped the old man to the nearest hospital. The old man thanked the boy and asked him for his name and address. The boy was ashamed to admit that his father was a poor fisherman, so he said, 'My name is Mustafa and my father is a teacher'. A few days later, the old man died in hospital, and left all his money to 'Mustafa, a local teacher's son who helped me in my hour of need'. Of course, because Ali had lied, he did not receive any of the old man's money.

Mark *five* places in the story where you could stop and ask students to predict what will happen next. What question would you ask each time? Practise telling the story to your partner.

B. Think of a story of your own. Practise telling it, pausing *every* now and then to ask what will happen next.

5   Lesson preparation

1. Plan a listening activity for a class. Either:
    – use an activity in the textbook; or
    – adapt a reading text for use as listening; or
    – tell the class a story; or
    – make a short recording of someone speaking English.
2. Decide what you would do *before*, *during* and *after* the listening stage.
    Think of ways of *helping* your students to listen and to focus their attention on the main points.

Self-evaluation sheet

Complete this after you have taught the lesson.

1. What was your listening activity? Briefly describe it.

2. What steps did you follow: before listening? after listening?

   before listening:

   after listening:

Think about these questions.

In general, how successful was the activity?
What did the students learn from it?

How much did the students understand the *first* time they listened?
How much more could they understand by the *end* of the activity?

Think of one student at the front of the class, one at the back, and one sitting by a window.
What were they each doing during the activity?
Could they understand? How do you know?

Think of one good student and one weaker student.
What did you do to keep each of them involved?
By the end of the activity, how do you think they each felt? Pleased with their progress? frustrated? interested? bored?

Think of the conditions in your classroom. Is there anything that makes listening difficult? (e.g. size, echo, noise from outside).
Could you improve the conditions in any way?

Did you use a cassette recorder?
If so, did you have any problems with:
– finding the place on the cassette?
– using the controls?
– finding the right sound level?
How could you overcome the problems next time?

18 Communicative activities

---

1 Introduction

A. Imagine you hear these conversations in real life. What might the situation be? Why is the person asking these questions?

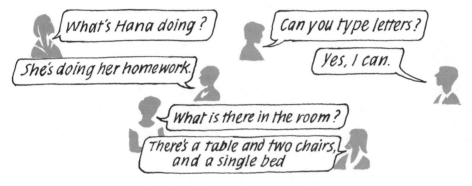

> What's Hana doing?
>
> She's doing her homework.

> Can you type letters?
>
> Yes, I can.

> What is there in the room?
>
> There's a table and two chairs, and a single bed

B. Imagine students in a class are asking and answering questions about this picture. What might they say? Why are they asking these questions?

2   Guessing games

A. Guess the picture

The teacher has a set of flashcards with simple pictures (e.g. clothes, food, places, actions). He or she chooses one card, but does *not* show it to the class. They must guess what it is by asking questions, e.g.:

T: Guess how I went to X.
Ss: Did you go by car?
      Did you go by bus?
      Did you walk?

B. Guess the sentence

The teacher writes a sentence on a piece of paper or card. He or she does not show the sentence, but writes the basic structure on the board, e.g.:

I went (somewhere) to (do something).

Students must guess the exact sentence by asking questions, e.g.:

Did you go to the park?
Did you go to school?
Did you go to the stadium?
Did you play football?
etc.

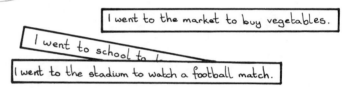

C. Mime

The teacher calls a student to the front and secretly gives her a sentence written on a piece of paper, which describes a simple activity. The student mimes the activity. The other students try to guess the situation.

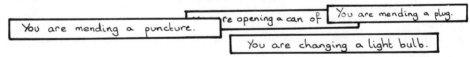

Here are two ways of organising guessing games in class. Which do you think is better? Why?

3 'Information gap' exercises

Here are some exercises for pairwork. In each pair, the two students are given
different information.

A.

STUDENT X	
This evening	
Tomorrow morning	
Tomorrow afternoon	
Tomorrow evening	

STUDENT Y

Tonight Kim is going
to stay at home, because
he wants to write a
letter to a friend.
Tomorrow morning he
has classes as usual
at college; but he
has the afternoon
free, so he's going
to help his father
repair the roof on
their house. In the
evening he's been
invited out to a
party.

B.

STUDENT X

Shopping list

2 packets tea
1 kilo sugar
1 Can orange juice
2 kilos rice
1 kilo beans
1 kilo oranges

STUDENT Y

YOU SELL:

tea   – 50p a packet
sugar   – 30p a kilo
rice   – 20p a kilo
orange juice – 25p a can

C. Find ten important differences.

4   Exchanging personal information

1. Work in pairs. Ask your partner questions about his or her daily routine.

Get up?	
Breakfast?	
School?	
Lunch?	
Evening?	
Go out?	

2. Think of another activity like this, using a grid. Choose a topic that students would find interesting.

5   Lesson preparation

1. Plan a communicative activity to include in a lesson. If possible, it should give further practice of language which is taught in the textbook. Choose one of these possibilities:
   − a guessing game
   − an 'information gap' exercise for pairwork or groupwork
   − an activity in which students exchange information about themselves
2. Plan the main steps you would follow in the activity, and prepare any materials you would need.

Self-evaluation sheet

Complete this after you have taught the lesson.

1. What kind of activity did you use? Briefly describe it.

2. What structures/vocabulary did it practise?

3. Write down the main steps you followed.

    a)

    b)

    c)

    d)

    e)

Think about these questions.

How long did the activity last?
Did it take longer or less time than you expected?

In general, how successful was the activity?
How did the students respond to it?
Were they: enthusiastic? interested? bored? confused? Why?

How much did students really communicate?

If you used a guessing game:
– How many students asked questions?
– How many students answered questions?
– What were the rest of the class doing during the activity?

If you used a pairwork or groupwork activity:
– How easy was it to: organise the pair/groupwork? explain what to do?
– How many students did the activity as you intended?
– What did the others do?

Do you think you will try an activity like this again?
Why / Why not?
How might you organise it differently next time?

19   Using English in class

1   Introduction

Think of your own lessons. In the activities below, do you normally use:
– mainly English?
– mainly the students' own language? ('L_1')
– a mixture of the two?

	English	L_1	Both
Introducing the lesson			
Checking attendance			
Organising where students sit			
Presenting new language			
Introducing a text			
Asking questions on a text			
Correcting errors			
Setting homework			

2   'Social' language

Here are some possible topics for 'chatting' to the class at the beginning or end of a lesson.

things students did the previous day

feast days and holidays

a piece of local news

a local sports event, e.g. a football match

a school performance (a play, concert, etc.)

a film on at
the cinema

an interesting
TV programme

birthdays

other topics?

1. What questions could you ask about each topic to encourage the students to talk?
· 2. Work in groups. Take it in turns to be 'teacher' – the rest of the group are your students. Choose one of the topics and 'chat' to your students.

3 'Organising' language

A. Look at the list of expressions the trainer will give you. Write a simple English equivalent for each one.

a) ....

b) ....

c) ....

d) ....

e) ....

f) ....

g) ....

h) ....

i) ....

j) ....

k) ....

B. Work in groups. What could you say in English in these situations?
   a) You are checking attendance.
   b) You are about to begin a new lesson in the book.
   c) The class have done some homework.
      – You are going through the answers together.
      – You want the students to correct each other's work.
      – You want to know how many had the correct answer.
   d) A student is not paying attention.
   e) The bell rings for the end of the lesson.

4 Giving simple explanations

Give one of these explanations as *simply* as you can in English. Imagine you are talking to people who speak very little English. Use gestures, drawings, and your own language to help!
a) Explain how to make a cake.
b) Explain how a mousetrap works.
c) Explain how to bandage a wound.
d) Explain everything you know about volcanoes.

5 English or your own language?

1. You want to teach these words.
    How would you explain their meaning:
    – using English only?
    – using English and your own language?

> skiing
> government
> liver

2. You want to teach these structures.
    How would you explain the difference:
    – using English only?
    – using English and your own language?

> How many | eggs | are there?
> | oranges |

> How much | bread | is there?
> | meat |

3. You are organising a role play. You want students to act out a conversation based on this situation.
    How would you explain the situation:
    – using English only?
    – using English and your own language?

> One student left his/her bag on a bus, containing some money, a book, and a towel. He/she goes to the lost property office.
>
> A second student is the person at the lost property office. He/she asks the student to describe the bag.

6   Lesson preparation

1. Look at a lesson you will teach soon, or find a lesson in a suitable textbook.
   Make a note of all the points in the lesson where you would have an
   opportunity to use English. Consider these possibilities:
   - 'chatting' at the beginning of the lesson
   - organising the students (arranging seating, calling students to the front,
     organising pairwork, etc.)
   - introducing the lesson
   - introducing topics, situations, texts
   - presenting words or structures
   - moving from one activity to another (saying what you will do next)
   - setting or marking homework
   - ending the lesson
2. Choose any *three* of these. Plan exactly what you would do and say.

Self-evaluation sheet   *Complete this after you have taught the lesson.*

What three things did you do 'in English'? Briefly describe them.

a)

b)

c)

Consider each of the three activities in turn. Think about these questions.

How much did you say in English? Can you remember what you said?
How much did the students say in English? Can you remember what they said?

How well did the class understand?
Did all the students understand? How do you know?
Did you need to: use gestures? use drawings? use your own language?

Was this the first time you used English for this part of the lesson?
If so:
- How did the class react?
- Would you use English in this way again? Why? / Why not?

20 Role play

1 Introduction

Look at these examples of role play activities.

a)

> One student imagines he/she is a
> farmer. Other students ask him/her
> questions about his/her daily routine.

b)

> A group of students imagine they are
> friends planning a holiday together.
> They try to decide where to go and
> what to do.

c)

> One student has lost a bag. He/she
> is at the police station reporting it to
> the police. The other student is the
> police officer, and asks for details.

Which activity would be the easiest for your students to do? Which would be the
most difficult? Why?
What other roles and situations would be suitable for role play activities in your
own class?

2   Improvising dialogues

1. What role play activities could be based on this dialogue?

Angela: Good morning. I want to send a letter to Singapore.
Clerk: Yes – do you want to send it air mail or ordinary mail?
Angela: I think I'll send it air mail. I want it to get there quickly. How much does it cost?
Clerk: To Singapore? That will be 30 pence, please.
Angela: (*gives the clerk 50 pence*) Here you are.
Clerk: Here's your stamp, and here's 20 pence change.
Angela: Thank you. Where's the post box?
Clerk: You want the air mail box. It's over there, by the door.

(adapted from *Living English* Book 2: A.G. Abdalla et al.)

2. Plan a similar role play based on a dialogue or text in your textbook.

3   Interviews based on a text

What role play activities could be based on these texts?

A.

If you met 15-year-old Jane Cole in the street, you might not notice anything special about her. But she is no ordinary schoolgirl, because as well as studying hard for her exams, she's training to take part in the European table tennis championship this summer. Jane will be one of the youngest contestants, but those who know her stamina and determination are confident that she will do well. Jane's main problem at the moment is finding time for both table tennis and schoolwork. For the last month, she's been getting up at six every day and doing an hour's table tennis practice before school; and then fitting in another hour in the afternoon.

B.

Edward caught the express train early in the morning. He was going to the next town to visit his relations. He had got up very early, and he felt tired, so he soon fell asleep. About an hour later, he woke up suddenly in the middle of a dream. In his dream, he was in a crowded tunnel. People were pushing him from all directions, and pulling at his clothes. As he woke up, he realised that it wasn't only a dream – somebody was really pulling at his coat pocket. He opened his eyes just in time to catch sight of a man slipping out of the compartment. His hand went to his pocket – his wallet was missing! He jumped up and ran into the corridor. But the man had vanished.

4   Free role play

1. Which of these topics are covered in the textbook you use?
   What other topics does the textbook cover?

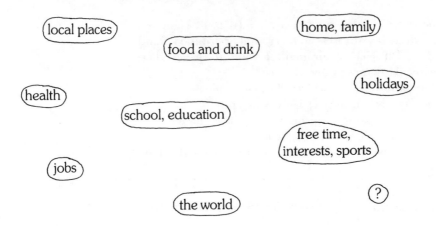

2. Choose *three* of the topics. For each one, think of suitable situations for free
   role play. Examples:

   Topic: School, education.
   Situation: You meet some foreign visitors to your country. They are
               interested in your school. Answer their questions about it.

   Topic: Health.
   Situation: A visitor to your town is ill. Find out what is the matter with
               him/her. Tell him/her where to find a doctor.

5   Lesson preparation

1. Choose a lesson you will teach soon, or find a lesson in a suitable textbook.
   Plan *either* a short role play activity based on a dialogue or text; *or* a free role
   play activity, using one of the topics covered in the lessons.
2. Decide exactly how you would organise the activity and what preparation
   would be necessary.

Self-evaluation sheet

Complete this after you have taught the lesson.

1. In your role play, what was the *situation*?

2. What *roles* did students take?

3. What *language* was practised?

   Structures:

   Vocabulary:

Think about these questions.

How long did the activity last?
Was it: long enough? too long? about right?

Did the students find the activity: interesting/boring? easy/difficult?
If there were difficulties, how might you overcome them next time?

How many students were actively involved in the role play?
What were the others doing?
Could you have involved more of the class? How?

Did the activity develop as you expected?
Did anything unexpected happen? If so, what?

What might you do differently next time you organise role play?

Background text: Preparing for communication

Our aim in practising oral English is to develop students' ability to communicate freely and spontaneously in English. To achieve this aim, we need to ask the following questions: What is real communication like? How is it different from the kind of controlled practice that usually takes place in language classes? How can we bring features of real communication into language practice?

Consider the two examples below. Conversation A shows a controlled exercise practising the structure 'should'; conversation B shows how the same structure might be used in real communication.

A. T: I feel tired.
   S: You should have a rest.
   T: I feel ill.
   S: You should see a doctor.
   T: I feel hungry.
   S: You should have a sandwich.

B. – I'd like to try and study in Britain for a few months. What do you think I should do?
   – Well, first of all you should go and see the British Council. They'll give you a list of language schools in Britain where you could go and study, and they'll also tell you if there are any ways of getting a grant or a scholarship. And then you could try . . .

As well as being at a more advanced level, there are several ways in which the language in B is different from that in A:
1. In B, the friend giving advice uses not just the single structure 'should', but a whole range of structures ('will', 'if', 'could', 'ways of . . . -ing'), expressing a variety of different functions (giving advice, making predictions, discussing possibilities). In order to communicate, he or she needs to know how to combine different structures together in context.
2. In B, the language is unpredictable. The friend uses the structure 'should', but he or she could have replied in many other ways: by using a different structure (e.g. 'If I were you . . .') or by giving a different response altogether (e.g. 'I've no idea' or 'What's the matter? Don't you like it here?'). To continue the conversation, the two speakers have to pay attention and respond to what the other person is saying. In A, the language is almost completely predictable; the responses are more or less fixed, and there is no chance for a conversation to develop.
3. In B, the speakers are using language for a purpose; there are things the first speaker does not know, and that is why he or she is asking the friend's advice. Although of course the speakers need to use structures correctly, their attention is focussed on conveying a message, on *what* they are talking about,

not on the language they are using. In A, the only reason for using language is to practise 'should' – the teacher is not really seeking advice or even pretending to. The practice is 'meaningful' in the sense that students must be aware of the meaning of what they are saying; but their attention is mainly focussed on 'getting the structure right', not on the message they are conveying. They do not even have the option of expressing the same message in a different way, e.g. 'Why not have a rest?'

4. The two friends in B are probably talking directly to each other in private; at most, there might be one or two other people listening to the conversation or taking part in it. It is private, face-to-face interaction; the two speakers react to each other and their personalities affect the way the conversation develops. In A, the 'conversation' is a public, formalised interaction, dominated by the teacher and with the whole class listening. There is nothing personal about the responses; they will be the same whichever student makes them.

This comparison highlights a considerable gap between traditional structural practice and the way we communicate in real life. This does not mean that traditional structural practice is therefore a waste of time; on the contrary, it is a very useful way of practising the structure 'should'. But it does suggest that this kind of practice *alone* will not prepare students very well for real communication in English. This might be achieved by giving practice which is controlled but which also includes some of the features of real communication. The analysis above suggests some ways in which this could be done:

– By giving practice involving more than just single sentences, so that students have a chance to use combinations of different functions and structures.
– By encouraging students to give a variety of responses, rather than insisting on one 'set' answer; by encouraging students to give personal responses; and by doing practice which naturally leads to unpredictable, creative language.
– By giving students a purpose for using language (e.g. through discussion, games, problem-solving, information gap activities); and by paying attention to what students are saying, not only to whether they are using language correctly.
– By organising activities in pairs and small groups, to give students the opportunity to use language in private, face-to-face interaction.

These activities will complement other more structure-based practice and should involve your students in real communication.

Discussion

Look at these examples of exercises and class activities:

Unit 1 Activity 4	Unit 18 Activities 2, 3 and 4
Unit 6 Activities 2 and 4	Unit 19 Activity 2
Unit 12 Activity 1	Unit 20 Activities 2, 3 and 4
Unit 14 Activity 3	

Do they include any of the features of real communication mentioned in the text? Which features?

21 Using worksheets

1 Introduction

A. Think about your textbook. Does it provide enough of each activity below?
Tick *Yes* or *No*.

	Yes	No
Controlled oral practice		
Free oral practice		
Reading		
Writing		
Grammar exercises		
Vocabulary development		

Now think about each activity again. Are the exercises in the textbook good
enough? How interesting are they? How well do they suit the students' needs?
Could they be improved in any way?

B.

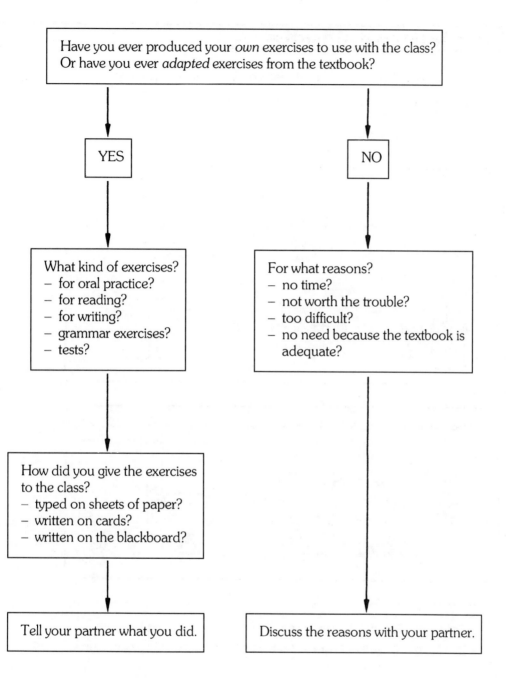

2   Worksheets for oral practice

Work in pairs. Try out each exercise. After each one, discuss the questions below.

1. What structures or vocabulary does this exercise practise?
2. What level of students is it suitable for?
3. How much time would it take?
4. What preparation would you need to do beforehand?

A.

The clothes shop is selling everything cheaply.
ASK AND ANSWER:
   How much is the ___? (...are the ___?)
   It was ___ pounds but now it's ___.
                              (They were ....).

B.

Ask and answer: What's he/she doing? What are they doing?
   He's ___ing. She's ___ing. They're ___ing.

C.

Find groups of three. Say how they are similar.
Example: Lions, tigers and giraffes are all African
         animals.

lion	Malaysia	tiger	maize	hotel
milk	screwdriver	lemonade	cinema	Pakistan
wheat	snake	frog	hammer	tea
giraffe	Japan	hospital	rice	lizard
saw				

3   Worksheets for reading and writing

Work through each exercise orally. After each one, discuss the questions below.

1. What level is the exercise?
2. What skills does it develop?
3. How clear are the instructions? Should they be in the students' own language?

A.

Match the two halves, (a) and (b).	
(a)	**(b)**
A pilot A nurse An engineer A farmer A librarian	designs machines takes care of books flies aeroplanes looks after sick people grows crops

B.

Copy the words in the correct order.

headlight   radiator
bumper   bonnet
tyre
windscreen
steering wheel

1._____.   5._____.
2._____.   6._____.
3._____.   7._____.
4._____.

C.

Write these words in alphabetical order:

green   great   gave

grapefruit   good

greatest   give

given   glove

D.

```
Copy the text, and add the missing words.

Your friend has fallen over and cut his/her knee. This is
what you should do: First, ........ your hands with soap and
water. Then, ........ at the cut and remove any ........ that
you can see there. Then ........ the cut with a little water -
but be careful, because it might ........ ! After that, take
a clean cloth and ........ the cut carefully. Finally, tie a
........ over the cut, to stop it getting dirty again.

        dirt    wash    dry
        look    clean   bandage
        hurt
```

4 Lesson preparation

1. Plan part of a lesson using worksheets for *either* oral practice *or* reading and
   writing. Use any of the worksheets which you or other teachers made in the
   training session, and if necessary adapt them to suit your own class.
   Either: Prepare copies of one worksheet, which will be used by all the
             students. Make enough copies for *every pair of students* in your class.
   Or: Prepare several different worksheets, which will be used at the same
             time by different students. Make several copies of *each* worksheet.

2. Plan the lesson carefully. Decide exactly how you would organise the activity
   and how long it would last.

Self-evaluation sheet   *Complete this after you have taught the lesson.*

1. How many worksheets did you use?

2. What skills did the worksheet(s) develop: speaking? reading? writing?

3. How long did the activity last?

4. Did students work: individually? in pairs? in groups?

Think about these questions.

Do you think the activity was: successful? fairly successful? not successful? Why?

How did you introduce the activity?
What instructions did you give? Did all the students understand them?

How many students could do the activity without help?
What mistakes did you notice? What did you do about them?

Did you have any problems in:
– making copies of the worksheet?
– giving the worksheets to the class?
– controlling the class during the activity?
– collecting the worksheets at the end?
How could you overcome them?

Do you think you will try using worksheets again?
Think of two reasons why or why not.

22 Classroom tests

1 What should we test?

We can test **language** (to find out what students have *learnt*):
– grammar
– vocabulary
– spelling
– pronunciation

We can test **skills** (to find out what students can *do*):
– listening
– reading
– speaking
– writing

Which of these are the most *important* for your students? Which are the *easiest* to test?

Imagine you are testing students to find out these things:
1. Can they follow street directions?
2. Can they form the past simple tense correctly?
3. Can they write a few sentences about their family?
4. Do they know common words for rooms and furniture?
5. Can they understand a simple description of their town?
Which main area would each test focus on?
Think of five questions like these about your own students.

2 Testing receptive skills

Read this text, and answer the questions.

> The dagona tree, which is common in the dry regions of Africa, has an unusual appearance. The fully-grown dagona is about twenty feet tall and has a thin trunk, about nine inches across. The trunk is bare for most of its height and the spiky branches, which have many small leaves, stand out from the top of the trunk, giving the tree the appearance of a large brush stuck in the ground.

The dagona tree has many uses. In October it produces large, round fruit with yellow flesh inside which can be eaten raw or made into a refreshing drink. The flesh can also be dried and made into flour. The outer skin of the fruit can be used for making glue; first it is dried, then the skin is pounded and mixed with water to make the glue. The bark of the tree is made up of fibres of great strength which are used to make ropes. And the spiky branches can be hollowed out and used as musical pipes.

(fictional description based on a text from *Reading for a purpose* Book 1: N.J.H. Grant and S.O. Unoh)

A. *True or false?*

Look at the following statements. Write T for true, F for false, and DK (don't know) if you can't tell from the text.

a) The dagona tree grows in Africa.
b) The dagona is common in rain forests.
c) The dagona produces fruit twice a year.
d) The flesh of the fruit can be used as a medicine.

B. *Multiple choice*

Choose the correct answer.

The dagona tree is: a) common in parts of Africa
                    b) found in sandy regions
                    c) common throughout the world
                    d) unusual in dry regions of the world

The tree looks like a brush because the branches:
                    a) are long and thin
                    b) are stuck in the ground
                    c) have many small leaves
                    d) grow out from the top of the trunk

C. *Open-ended questions*

Give short answers to these questions.

What does the fruit look like?
The fruit has four uses. What are they?
Why is the bark good for making ropes?

≫→

D. *Information transfer*
Complete this table.

Part of tree	Use
a) flesh of fruit	food, drink, flour
b) skin of fruit	
c)	
d)	

What are the good and bad points of each type of question?

3   Testing grammar and writing

Look at these tests.
Which ones mainly test *grammar*?
Which ones mainly test *writing skills*?
Number them from 1 to 5 according to how
much they focus on grammar or writing
(1 = grammar, 5 = writing).

A.
Give the past tense forms of these
verbs:
    meet   go   come   see
    hear   take

B.
What did you do before you came here today?

Write *three* sentences.

C.
Write these notes as full sentences. Put the verbs into the
correct form.

I/spend/last week/try/find/job.
I/buy/newspaper/look/advertisements.
I/see/interesting/job/shoe factory.
I/go/interview/but/not/get/job.

D.

> Fill in the gaps with suitable verbs.
>
> Yesterday John _____ lunch in a restaurant. Then he _____ his friend Peter and they _____ to a football match together. When they arrived, they _____ thirsty, so they _____ some lemonade.

E.

> Fill the gaps with a suitable word or phrase.
>
> 1. I feel so tired! I _____ at five o'clock this morning.
> 2. There used to be a cinema in the town, but it _____ last month.
> 3. When I was a boy, we _____ a large house by the sea.

4 Marking free writing tests

Here are two students' answers to Test B in the last activity. Work in pairs. Give each answer a mark out of ten.

thes moor meeng , I have bookfes and I get up a 7.30 Am
I have go to studeng only 5 menuts and after I have gone
to the school .

This morning I got up AT six o'clock. and I had
to readed per one hour in my room.
At HALf pasT six I had To went in The Park.
After I had come at the school on foot
It was raining.
Now I'm going To lunch

5   Oral tests

Imagine you are giving short oral tests to your students (one minute each).
Which of these topics would be suitable?

a) Talk about yourself and your family.
b) Ask the teacher some questions.
c) Describe your village/town.
d) Talk about a friend.
e) Talk about your school.
f) Talk about transport in your region.

Think of five other topics that you could use, and write them down.

....

....

....

....

....

6   Lesson preparation

Prepare a test to give to your class. The test should focus on *one* of these skills:
reading, listening, writing or speaking. Use any of the techniques you have
discussed in this unit.
Note: If you are giving a reading or listening test, you should use a text that the
students do *not* know.

Self-evaluation sheet

Complete this after you have given the test.

1. Which skill did you test: reading? writing? listening? speaking?

2. Briefly describe what happened in the test.

Think about these questions.

In general, how successful was the test?
What were its good points?
What were its bad points?

Did it seem to have a positive or a negative effect on the students' learning?

Could most students do the test easily?
How did they react to it?

What did you learn from the test about your students' ability?
Did anything surprise you?
What did the students learn about their ability?

How did you prepare the class for the test?
Did you need to help them during the test? If so, in what way?
What did you do after the test?

Would you give the class a test like this again?
If so, what improvements might you make?

23   Planning a week's teaching

1   Learning activities

Work in groups. Look at each of these activities in turn. Try to think about them
from the *student's* point of view. Discuss:
1. For what *stage* of the lesson is the activity suitable?
2. How *valuable* is the activity? What do students learn from it?
3. Is the activity suited to one *level* (e.g. first year students) more than others?
4. How often do students do this activity in your class?

Learning activity (activities done in class)	Stage	Learning value A/B/C/D/E	Level	Your class?
Listening to a text				
Answering questions on a text				
Reading aloud				
Silent reading				
Repetition drills				
Substitution drills				
Question/answer practice (whole class)				
Oral practice in pairs				
Guessing games				
Copying words/sentences				
Dictation				
Paragraph writing				
Role play				

Learning activity	Stage	Value	Level	Your class?
Free discussion of a topic				
Correcting each other's written work				

Look at the list again. Which activities could you include in a series of lessons you might teach soon?

2   Teaching techniques

Here are two different ways of using a reading text.

Teacher A

1. Introduces the text with a short discussion of the topic.
2. Gives a guiding question. Reads the text. Students listen while reading, then answer the question.
3. Presents new words, using examples in English.
4. Asks a series of questions on the text. Students give short answers.
5. Asks a few personal questions based on the text.

Teacher B

1. Reads out a vocabulary list from the book. Students repeat in chorus.
2. Reads the text aloud sentence by sentence. Students repeat.
3. Students read the text aloud round the class.
4. Asks questions from the book, and gives the answers. Students repeat in chorus.
5. Asks the same questions again. Students answer round the class.

What are the main differences in the teachers' techniques?
What do you think the students would *learn* from each of these lessons?

3   Teaching aids

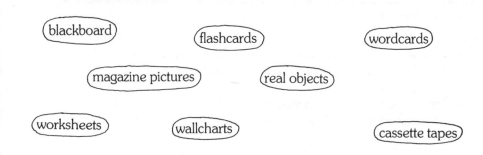

Which of these teaching aids have you used in your own class?
How useful are they? What activities can they be used for?
Which ones could you use in a series of lessons you might teach soon?

4   Types of interaction

What kind of interaction is shown in each picture?

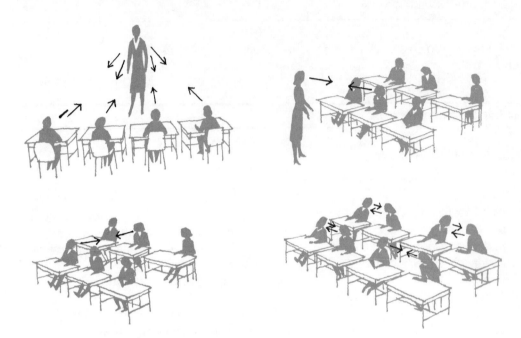

What kind of interaction would be suitable for each activity below?
   drills
   question/answer practice
   answering questions on a text
   role play
   guessing games
   correcting written exercises

5   Lesson preparation

1. Write a plan for next week's lessons (or for any series of five or six lessons
   which you will teach in the future). Try to include a *variety* of activities and
   techniques. Include in your plan:
   – the aim of each lesson and the main language taught in it;
   – details of activities and techniques which you would add to those suggested
     in the textbook;
   – different types of interaction you plan to use;
   – any teaching aids you could use.

2. In your classes, try to keep to the plan you have made.

Self-evaluation sheet

Complete this at the end of the week's teaching.

Write down the aim of each lesson, and the main language you taught in it.

Lesson 1:

Lesson 2:

Lesson 3:

Lesson 4:

Lesson 5:

Lesson 6:

Think about these questions.

How closely did you follow your plan?
At what points did you depart from it?

Think about the aims of the lessons. How well did each lesson achieve its aim?
Think about the vocabulary and structures you taught.
How successfully did students seem to *learn* them?

What activities in the lessons developed: speaking? listening? reading? writing?
Which skill was developed most?
Did you feel that you neglected any of the skills?

Did you include any *new* activities or techniques in the lessons?
If so, how successful were they?
Will you include any of them in future lessons? Why / Why not?

In general, did planning your week's teaching improve the lessons?
Was it worth the time spent on it?

24 Self-evaluation

1 Good and bad teaching

Good teaching

1. Work with a partner. Try to agree on *five* important characteristics of good teaching. Write them down.

   a)

   b)

   c)

   d)

   e)

2. Now choose the one you think is *most* important.
3. Evaluate yourself. How far are these five characteristics true of your own teaching?

Bad teaching

1. With your partner, try to agree on *five* important characteristics of bad teaching. Write them down.

   a)

   b)

   c)

   d)

   e)

2. Choose the one you think is *most* harmful.
3. Evaluate yourself again. How far are these five characteristics true of your own teaching?

2   Categories for observation

A Teaching procedure
B Use of teaching aids
C Involvement of the class
D Teacher's personality
E Command of English

Look at the questions below.
– Which category does each question belong to? Write a letter beside the
  question.
– How important is each question? Write a number from 0 (= not important) to
  5 (= very important).

	Category	How important?
1. Is the aim of the lesson clear?		
2. Does the teacher write clearly on the board?		
3. Do students participate actively in the lesson?		
4. Does the teacher do a variety of activities?		
5. Are the stages of the lesson clear?		
6. Does the teacher have clear pronunciation?		
7. Does the teacher smile often?		
8. Does the teacher use visuals appropriately?		
9. Does the teacher speak naturally?		
10. Does the teacher encourage students to ask questions?		
11. Does the teacher encourage real use of language?		
12. Does the teacher seem interested in the lesson?		

3   Classroom climate

Look at these statements. Each one describes a teacher's behaviour in class.
Which of them would have a *good* effect on the classroom climate? Which would
have a *bad* effect?

a) The teacher corrects *every* error.
b) The teacher *hardly ever* corrects errors.
c) The teacher lets students know who is first, second, last, etc. in the class.
d) The teacher praises students who answer correctly.
e) The teacher criticises students who repeatedly make mistakes.
f) The teacher punishes students who behave badly.
g) The teacher usually chooses good students to answer.
h) The teacher often chooses weaker students to answer.
i) The teacher uses only English in the lesson.
j) The teacher mostly uses English in the lesson.
k) The teacher translates everything into the students' own language.

4   The students

Think about *one* of the classes you have taught.
Are there any students who:
– find the lessons very easy?
– have difficulty understanding the lessons?
– are very quiet or unwilling to participate?
– are difficult to control?
– have difficulty seeing or hearing?
– have problems with reading or writing their own language?

Work with a partner. Tell your partner about them and discuss what you could do
to help them and keep them involved in the class.

5   Lesson preparation

Plan a complete lesson. Try to include a variety of activities, and to use some of
the techniques introduced in this training course.
Include in your plan:
– the aims of the lesson;
– the main stages of activity;
– detailed notes for each stage.

Self-evaluation sheet

Answer these questions after you have taught the lesson.
Write brief notes on a separate sheet of paper.

Preparation

1. How useful was your lesson plan? Were you able to follow it or did you have to depart from it during the lesson?
2. What difficulties did you find in planning the lesson?
3. Now that you have taught your lesson, what changes would you make to the plan for the next time?

Your teaching

1. How successful was the lesson?
2. Which part of the lesson was most successful? Why?
3. Which part of the lesson was least successful? Why?
4. How did you ensure that all the students understood?
5. How much did you use the blackboard? Was it effective?
6. What other aids did you use? Were they effective?
7. Which of the four skills did you develop most?
8. How much did you use the students' own language? Should you have used more or less?
9. What aspect of the lesson gave you most difficulty? Why?
10. How was this lesson different from the one you taught before and after it?

The students

1. What activities did the students enjoy most? Why?
2. What did the students find the most difficult? Why?
3. Did any students fail to participate? If so, why was this?
4. What discipline problems were there? What caused them? How did you deal with them?
5. What advice might the students give *you* about the lesson?

This unit incorporates ideas suggested by Stephen Gaies, University of Northern Iowa.

Summaries

Unit 1: Presenting vocabulary

Presenting new vocabulary involves: showing the form of the word (how it is pronounced and spelt); showing the meaning of the word clearly; giving students a chance to hear how the word is used.

Some ways of showing the meaning of a word:
1. **Using visuals:**
   - *Real objects:* things in the classroom, things you can bring into the classroom, yourself and your students.
   - *Pictures:* blackboard drawings, pictures from magazines, pictures you have drawn yourself before the lesson.
   - Actions, mime, facial expressions.
2. **Giving examples** to make the meaning clear.
3. **Using the students' own language:** This is often the easiest and clearest way to show the meaning of a word; but give an example in English first so that students can hear how the word is used.

Some ways of involving the class and checking that they understand:
- Instead of giving a direct translation of a word, give an example and then let the class guess what the word means.
- Use the word in simple questions. This gives the class a chance to hear the word in context and react to it.

Unit 2: Asking questions

Question types:
1. **Yes/No questions:**
   'Is she English?' 'No, she isn't.'
   'Did you bring some food?' 'Yes, I did.'
2. **'Or' questions:**
   'Is she English or German?' 'German.'
   'Is your room at the front or the back?' 'At the front.'
3. **WH- questions:**
   'When did he arrive?' 'Yesterday morning.'
   'How many people are there here?' 'About fifty.'
All these questions naturally have *short* answers. If your aim is to check comprehension, there is no need for students to answer with a complete

sentence. To elicit a long answer naturally:
– Ask a more general question: What did they do first? Then what happened?
– 'Prompt' an answer: Tell me about (your home town). What about (shops)?

Questioning strategies:
A basic strategy for asking questions:
– Ask first, then pause to give students time to think, then choose a student to answer. Do not always let 'good' students answer; try to involve weaker and shyer students.

Unit 3: Presenting structures

To show the meaning of a structure, you can:
– show the meaning directly, using things the students can see in the classroom (objects; your face, clothes, actions; the students; pictures);
– give examples from real life (your own life, students' lives, your town, etc.);
– invent a situation and give imaginary examples.

A basic procedure for presenting a structure:
1. Give one or two examples to show what the structure means.
2. Say the structure and ask students to repeat it.
3. Write an example on the board.
4. Give other situations and examples.

To involve the class as much as possible:
– Think of interesting situations and examples.
– Ask questions during your presentation.
– Get students to tell you what to write on the board.
– Get students to give examples of the structure.

Unit 4: Using the blackboard

Writing on the blackboard:
– Stand sideways and write with your arm extended, so that students can see the board.
– Talk as you write. To involve the class more, ask students to tell you what to write next.
– Decide before the lesson how to organise the blackboard clearly. Leave the centre free for writing the main structures; write vocabulary in a list at the side.

Show structures clearly by **underlining**, or by means of **tables**:

He works in an office.

I work		bank
	in a	
She works		factory

》》→

Use the board to write **prompts** for practice:

flour	½ kilo	
rice	2 kilos	'How much .... do we need?'
oil	1 bottle	'We need ....'
sugar	2 packets	

For examples of **blackboard drawings**, see pages 16 and 17.

Unit 5: Using a reading text

A possible procedure for reading a text:
1. Introduce the text, and present essential new vocabulary.
2. Give one or two guiding questions for students to think about as they read.
3. Let students read the text silently, then check answers to guiding questions.
4. Ask questions on the text to check comprehension, and explain any new words.
5. If the text is suitable, use it as a basis for further language practice.

Vocabulary: You do not need to present all the new vocabulary beforehand. Encourage students to guess the meaning of unknown words as they read the text.

Introducing the text: This is to help the students read and to increase their interest – so do not give too much information about the text.

Silent reading: If you let students read the text silently to themselves:
– they have a chance to read at their own speed and think about the meaning of the text;
– it gives them practice in reading alone, without hearing the words they read (this is the skill they need to develop).

Checking comprehension:
– Ask short, simple questions which will help to focus attention on the text.
– Encourage students to give short answers (to show whether they have understood the text).
– Let students keep their books open, so that they can refer to the text to answer the questions.

Unit 6: Practising structures

Types of drill:
1. *Repetition:* The teacher gives examples of a structure; students repeat them.
2. *Substitution:* The teacher gives prompts; students give examples of the structure using the prompt. (For examples, see Activity 1.)

Structure practice can be either **mechanical** or **meaningful**:

Mechanical practice: Students can do the practice correctly without thinking about meaning. The focus is entirely on the form of the structure.

Meaningful practice: Students must think and understand what they are saying in order to do the practice. Ways of making practice meaningful:
– Get students to say real things about themselves.
– Give a situation which suggests a certain structure but leaves the student to choose exactly what to say.
– Let students add something of their own.
For examples, see Activity 2.

Ways of involving the class in structure practice:
– Do the practice quickly, getting responses from different students in turn.
– In question/answer practice, get students to ask each other questions.
– For freer practice, give a few minutes' preparation time, so that students can think of things to say.

Unit 7: Using visual aids

Real objects can be used:
– to teach vocabulary (e.g. a bag of sugar, a packet of tea);
– to practise a structure (e.g. 'I'm going to make some tea');
– to develop a description or a story (e.g. giving instructions for making tea);
– to develop a dialogue (e.g. 'How much is a packet of tea?' '50 pence.').

Flashcards: Cards with simple pictures (or words or numbers) can be held up by the teacher or given out to students to use in pair and groupwork. Flashcards can be used:
– to teach vocabulary (e.g. pictures of knife, fork, spoon, plate, cup);
– to practise structures (e.g. pictures of different activities to practise 'Do you like writing letters?', 'Do you like swimming?', etc.).
Making flashcards: use half a sheet of typing paper, or a piece of card; draw the picture with a thick black pen, or cut pictures from a magazine.

Charts: Larger sheets of paper or card – the teacher can hold them up or display them on the wall or the blackboard.
Charts can be used to show:
– a series of pictures that tell a story;
– a table of structures (e.g. verb tenses);
– a diagram showing a process (e.g. how something is made).

Unit 8: Planning a lesson

Before starting a lesson, it is important to know:
– the aim of the lesson;
– the new language to be taught in the lesson;
– the main stages of the lesson;
– what to do at each stage.

⟫→

Aims and content of the lesson: The lesson may focus on a particular topic (e.g. sports), a particular structure (e.g. practice of 'going to') or a skill (e.g. understanding spoken instructions). When thinking of the aim, ask: What should the students learn to do in this lesson?

Main stages of the lesson:
Presentation: The teacher presents new words and structures.
Practice: Students practise words and structures in a controlled way.
Production: Students use language they have learnt to express themselves more freely.
(Practice and production can be oral or written.)
Reading: Students read a text and answer questions or do a task (e.g. completing a table).
Listening: Students listen to a text or dialogue, on cassette or read by the teacher.
(These stages are not in a fixed order.)

Unit 9: Teaching basic reading

When students read, they need to *recognise* words and sentences and *understand* them. In the early stages, they may find it helpful to *say* the words as they read them, but this is not an essential part of reading. To help students to read, we need to give them practice in understanding written sentences; the emphasis should be on understanding meaning, not on repeating sentences aloud or on spelling out words.

It is easier for students to recognise words if they see them in sentences, because they can guess the words from the context. So it will help students if we let them read complete sentences as early as possible.

Some techniques for practising reading:
Look and say: The teacher shows words and phrases on cards. Students look at them and say the words. This gives word recognition practice for beginners.
Read and do: Students read simple instructions, and do what the instructions tell them.
Read and choose: Students look at a picture and read sentences. They choose the sentence which correctly describes the picture.
Read and match: Sentences are split into two halves. Students read them and match the halves together.
For examples, see Activities 2 and 3.

Unit 10: Teaching pronunciation

Sounds: To help students with a difficult sound:
1. Say the sound clearly, show how it is pronounced in different words and get students to repeat them.
2. Contrast the sound with other, similar sounds.
3. Describe how the sound is produced, if you can do this easily.

Stress: Most English words have one stressed syllable and two or more unstressed syllables. The vowel in the unstressed syllable is usually **reduced**; it is pronounced as /ə/ or /ɪ/: apart, vegetable, Monday, between.

In connected speech, more vowels become reduced because complete words are unstressed: There were a lot of people at the party.

Ways of showing stress patterns: say the sentence, exaggerating the stressed syllables; use arm gestures; clap your hands; write dots and dashes on the board: (he was late = • • —).

Intonation: Basic intonation patterns:
1. *Rising tune:* The voice rises on the stressed syllable. Used in Yes/No questions, and to express surprise or uncertainty.
2. *Falling tune:* The voice rises earlier in the sentence, then falls on the last stressed syllable. Used for normal sentences and most WH- questions.

Using 'back-chaining' to practise intonation: ask students to repeat the sentence in sections, starting with the end and working back to the complete sentence.

Unit 11: Teaching handwriting

Styles of handwriting:
1. **Printing:** the letters are separate and look the same as in printed books.
2. **Simple cursive:** most letters are joined, but they keep the same shapes as in printing.
3. **Full cursive:** all the letters are joined, and many letters have different shapes from printing. For examples, see Activity 1.

A basic procedure for teaching a new letter:
– Write the letter on lines on the board; describe how it is formed in simple English or the students' own language.
– Students copy it several times separately along a line in their books.

Joining letters: Joins are made from the end of one letter to the beginning of the next (not always the closest point). Practise joining common combinations only (e.g. *ta, te, th, nt,* but not *tg, dt*).

Techniques for copying words:
– *'Delayed copying':* The teacher writes a word on the board; the students read it but do not write. The teacher erases the word and students write it. This ensures that students are thinking of the whole word, not just a series of letters.
– *'Meaningful copying':* Students do a simple reading task (e.g. matching words together, matching words with pictures, putting words in the correct order) and then copy the answer. This ensures that students understand what they are copying. For examples, see Activity 4.

Unit 12: Pairwork and groupwork

Pairwork: The teacher divides the whole class into pairs; all the pairs work at the same time.
Groupwork: The teacher divides the class into small groups to work together (usually four or five students in each group).

Advantages of pair and groupwork:
– It gives students more opportunity to speak English.
– All the students are involved in the activity.
– Shy students feel more secure and are more willing to speak.
– It encourages students to share ideas and help each other.

Overcoming problems:
– *Students' mistakes:* Give preparation before the activity, and check afterwards by asking some students what they said.
– *Controlling the class:* Give clear instructions about what to do and when to start and stop. Give clearly defined tasks which do not go on too long.

Suitable activities for pair and groupwork:
Controlled oral practice: can be done with the whole class first, then in pairs.
Reading a text: students read the text silently, then discuss questions in pairs.
Writing exercises: students work in groups, deciding together what to write; one student acts as 'secretary'.
Free discussion: can be done in groups. Define the discussion first, and give a clear purpose.

Unit 13: Writing activities

Controlled writing can be made more meaningful and interesting by:
– letting students add something of their own instead of just copying;
– giving tasks that make students think about what they are writing.
For examples of controlled writing exercises, see Activity 1.

Disadvantages of dictation: it can be done mechanically without real comprehension; it takes up a lot of time in class; it practises spelling more than sentence writing skills.
An alternative to dictation: reconstructing a text from prompts. The teacher writes prompts on the board, then reads the text while the students listen. Then students write a version of the text, based on the prompts.

If students move straight from controlled exercises to completely free writing, they are likely to make many mistakes, and so find writing frustrating. Free writing is also time-consuming for the teacher, because students usually write completely different paragraphs which have to be corrected individually. These problems can be overcome by giving **guided writing** activities. Ways of guiding writing:

Writing based on a text: Students read a short text, then write a paragraph which is similar but which involves some changes.

Oral preparation: The teacher prepares orally with the class, getting suggestions from students, and writing key expressions on the board. Students use this as a basis for their writing. For examples, see Activities 2 and 3.

Unit 14: Eliciting

At the presentation stage of the lesson, the teacher has two alternatives:
– To **present** language or a situation directly; the teacher does most of the talking, while the students listen.
– To **elicit**; the teacher asks students for ideas and suggestions, and gets them to guess and to say what they know already.

Eliciting is a useful way of involving the class by focussing students' attention and making them think; it establishes what students know and what they do not know; and it encourages students to make guesses and to work out rules for themselves.

Eliciting from pictures: Pictures provide good opportunities to elicit language. The teacher can:
– ask students to describe the picture;
– ask students to interpret things which are not clear in the picture;
– ask students to imagine things beyond the picture.

Eliciting technique:
1. Pause after asking a question, to give all students time to think.
2. If there is more than one possible answer, encourage a range of answers from different students.
3. Elicit vocabulary or structures 'onto the blackboard', writing as students make suggestions.

Unit 15: Reading activities

Before students read a text, we can organise a **pre-reading activity**, to arouse their interest in the topic and make them want to read. The activity should encourage them to think about the topic and to make predictions and guesses about what they will read. For examples, see Activity 1.

Questions on a text: Questions should check comprehension and also help students to read the text by focussing their attention on the main points. To achieve this, all the students should be involved in answering the questions and know why answers are right or wrong. Ways of involving the class:
– Ask students to write short answers to the questions, then discuss them together.

⟫→

– Divide students into groups to discuss the questions, then go through the answers together.

Asking questions is not the only way to check comprehension. We can also ask students to do a simple **reading task**: for example, students read the text and note down information in a table (see Activity 3).

As well as straightforward comprehension questions, we can ask questions that require students to **respond** to the text. Possible question types:
– Asking students to match what they read against their own experience.
– Asking students to imagine a situation related to the text.
– Asking students to express feelings or opinions (see Activity 4).

Unit 16: Correcting errors

Spoken errors: When students are doing controlled practice, we are usually concerned with accuracy; so we need to correct important errors as they occur. When students are involved in freer activity (e.g. discussion, role play), we want them to develop fluency; so it is better not to interrupt by correcting too often, but to remember common errors and deal with them afterwards.
Possible techniques for correcting errors:
– Give the correct form; the student repeats it.
– Indicate where the error is, but let the student correct himself or herself.
– Pass the question on to another student, then give the first student a chance to repeat the correct form.
To help students develop a positive attitude to errors: encourage them, focussing on what they have got right, and praise them for correct and partly correct answers, so that they feel they are making progress.

Written errors: To avoid too much correction of written work, give simple writing tasks which will not lead to many mistakes and which can be corrected in class. Correcting work in class:
– Go through the answers, writing on the board only if spelling is a problem.
– Let students correct their own work or exchange books and correct each other's.
– Move round the class to check what they are doing.

Unit 17: Listening activities

Two ways of helping to focus students' attention during listening:
– Give a simple listening **task**, e.g. a table of information for students to complete as they listen.
– Give one or two **guiding questions** before the listening; students listen and find the answers.

To help students listen:
– Introduce the topic beforehand, so that students are able to predict what they might hear.
– Divide the listening into stages:
  i) students listen for main idea;
  ii) students listen again for details.
– If the listening text is long, divide it into sections, and check comprehension after each section.

Using a cassette recorder for intensive listening:
– Play the whole text and check general comprehension.
– Play part of the text again, pausing after particular remarks to see if students could 'catch' what was said. If necessary, rewind the cassette a little way and play the remark again.

Unit 18: Communicative activities

In real life, we usually talk in order to tell people things they do not already know, or to find out things from other people; we have a **reason** to communicate, a 'communicative need'. In classroom activities, we can create a similar need to communicate by introducing an 'information gap' – some students have information that others do not have, so there is a reason to talk and ask questions.

Guessing games: The teacher or a student at the front has a picture or a sentence, which the class cannot see. Students guess what it is by asking questions. Guessing games can also be organised in groups; one student in each group has the information, the others guess. For examples of guessing games, see Activity 2.

Information gap exercises for pairwork: Students work in pairs. To create a communicative need, the two students in each pair are given different information. For examples of information gap exercises, see Activity 3.

Exchanging personal information: Students work in pairs, and exchange information about their own lives, interests, experiences, etc. As they listen, they make notes about their partner, using a grid. There is a natural 'information gap', because every student has slightly different experiences and interests. For an example, see Activity 4.

Unit 19: Using English in class

English can be used in teaching the lesson itself: giving examples, introducing a text, asking questions, etc. It can also be used for activities which 'surround' the lesson: checking attendance, telling students where to sit, controlling the class, 'chatting' to students, etc.

Advantages of using English in class:
– Students have more practice in listening to natural spoken English.
– It gives students the feeling of English as a real language used for communication, not just a language in a textbook.

Opportunities to use English:
– *'Social' language:* 'chatting' in English at the beginning of the lesson. This creates an 'English language' atmosphere in the class, establishes contact between teacher and students, and helps students to feel relaxed. For suitable topics for 'social' language, see Activity 2.
– *'Organising' language:* e.g. starting and stopping activities, getting students to do and not to do things. Much of this consists of simple instructions which are repeated lesson after lesson, and can easily be given in English.
– *Giving explanations:* English can be used for explaining how an activity works, or explaining a new word or grammar point. To be effective, the explanation should be as clear and simple as possible; the teacher can help students understand by using gestures, drawings on the blackboard, and repeating words in the students' own language.

Unit 20: Role play

In role play, students imagine a **role** (e.g. a police officer, a shop assistant), a **situation** (e.g. buying food, planning a party), or both. Role play should be **improvised**: students decide exactly what to say as they go along.

Controlled role play:
– *Role play based on a dialogue in the textbook:* After practising the dialogue, ask pairs of students in turn to improvise similar dialogues; or divide the class into pairs and let all the students improvise at the same time.
– *Role play interview based on a text:* Ask one student to take the role of a character from the text. Other students ask him or her questions.

Free role play:
– *Prepared in class:* Discuss with the whole class what the speakers might say, and write prompts on the board. Let all the students practise the role play in pairs first. Then ask one or two good pairs to perform the role play in front of the class.
– *Prepared at home:* Divide the class into groups. Give each group a different situation and roles. Each group prepares their role play outside the class, in their own time. Groups perform their role plays in turn, on different days.

Unit 21: Using worksheets

Worksheets are exercises written or typed on sheets of paper and given out to the class. They can be used for oral practice or for reading and writing. Some uses of worksheets:

- To supplement exercises in the textbook which are inadequate or unsuitable for the class.
- To help the teacher organise a class in a particular way (e.g. students working alone at their own speed).
- To make a change from the textbook and add variety to the lesson.

Worksheets for oral practice: One worksheet can be given to each pair of students. They work through the exercise(s) in pairs, then the teacher discusses the answers with the whole class. For examples of exercises, see Activity 2.

Worksheets for reading and writing can be used in two ways:
- Copies of the same worksheet can be given to every student; all the students do the activity at the same time, working alone or in pairs. Then the teacher goes through the answers, or students correct each other's work.
- The teacher can build up a set of different worksheets, with several copies of each. Different students use different worksheets in the same lesson; this allows students to work at their own level and speed.

For examples of exercises, see Activity 3.

Unit 22: Classroom tests

Regular informal tests are useful because they tell the teacher what students can and cannot do, and therefore how successful his or her teaching has been; and they tell the students how well they are progressing, and give them definite goals in their learning. To comment accurately on a student's progress, we need to test his or her ability in each of the four skills (speaking, listening, reading, writing) as well as his or her knowledge of grammar and vocabulary.

Testing receptive skills (reading and listening): Questions should test comprehension of the main points, and should genuinely test comprehension (so it should not be possible to guess the answers); they should be easy to set and to mark. Types of question: True/False/Don't know; Multiple choice; Open-ended; Information transfer. For examples, see Activity 2.

Testing grammar and writing: If we want to encourage students to improve their writing, we need to test writing skills, not just knowledge of grammar. It is usually easiest to give controlled writing tests; free writing tests are difficult and time-consuming to mark. For examples of controlled writing tests, see Activity 3.

Testing speaking: We can test speaking by:
- *Continuous assessment:* The teacher gives a mark for participation over a series of lessons.
- *Short oral tests:* The teacher calls each student out in turn and tests him or her on a prepared topic. Each test lasts 30–60 seconds.

Unit 23: Planning a week's teaching

To maintain the interest of the class, it is important to include a variety of activities and techniques; to do this, we need to think beyond individual lessons and plan teaching and learning over a longer period.

Learning activities: When planning to introduce a variety of activities, we need to know:
- What is the learning value of each activity? (How much do students learn from it? How much time is worth spending on it?)
- What skills does it develop? (Reading? Writing? Listening? Speaking? More than one skill?)
- What stage of the lesson is it suitable for? (e.g. Presentation? Practice? Review?)

Teaching techniques: The same activity can be done in many different ways. The success of an activity depends partly on the teaching techniques we use. So when planning an activity we need to consider:
- what 'teaching steps' to follow;
- what aids and materials to use and how to use them;
- what different kinds of interaction to use (e.g. pairwork, individual work).

Unit 24: Self-evaluation

Self-evaluation: the ability of a teacher to judge his or her own teaching honestly and to see how much learning is taking place in the class. For teachers to evaluate themselves, they need to observe themselves. They can do this indirectly by careful planning before the lesson, followed by reflection after the lesson on what took place.

Teaching is a three-way relationship between the teacher, the materials he or she is using (e.g. the textbook), and the students. When observing teaching (or evaluating our own teaching) it is useful to focus on one aspect of this relationship at a time. For examples of categories which can be used in observation, see Activity 2.

The purpose of teaching is to help students to learn, so we can only judge teaching by seeing how well students succeed in learning. The teacher can improve students' chances of learning by:
- Creating a good 'classroom climate': The classroom climate is affected by the teacher's own attitude and behaviour, e.g. how he or she deals with errors, how he or she controls the class, how much he or she uses English in the lesson.
- Being sensitive to the needs of individual learners, and recognising that each student has different needs and problems. So the teacher should try to find out more about each student, e.g. by getting them to talk and write about themselves, and by finding time to talk to students outside the class.

Acknowledgements

The authors and publishers are grateful to the following for permission to reproduce copyright material. It has not been possible to contact the copyright holders of all the material used and in such cases the publishers would welcome further information.

Longman Group Ltd for the lesson based on an extract from the *Nile Course for the Sudan* Book 3 by M. Bates on p. 13, and for the table based on an extract from *Welcome to English* Book 1 by M. Bates and J. Higgens on p. 34; R. Leakey and Hamish Hamilton Ltd for the extract from *Human Origins* on p. 18; H. M. Abdoul-Fetouh et al and the Ministry of Education, Cairo, Egypt for the texts based on an extract from *Living English* Book 3 on p. 32; S. Steel and A & C Black (Publishers) Ltd for the text from *Earthquakes and Volcanoes* (Junior Reference series) on p. 72; T. and J. Watson and Wayland (Publishers) Ltd for the extracts from *What the World Eats – Midday Meal* on p. 75; A. G. Abdalla et al and the Ministry of Education, Cairo, Egypt for the dialogue based on an extract from *Living English* Book 2 on p. 101.

Photographs and illustrations:
Christina Gascoigne for the photograph from the New Internationalist Calendar (February) 1986 on p. 67; BBC Hulton Picture Library for the photograph on p. 71; P. Beasant and Usborne Publishing Ltd for the illustration with text from the *Young Scientist Book of Medicine* on p. 74.

Drawings by Jackie Barnett, Leslie Marshall and Alexa Rutherford
Book design by Peter Ducker MSTD